Glory Wind Beneath My Wings

Regina G. Mixon

Glory Wind Beneath My Wings

All Rights Reserved
ISBN 978-0-9820699-2-9
Published by:
REGS Books, LLC
P. O. Box 5397
Torrance, CA 90510
www.regsbooks.org

No part of this publication may be reproduced, stored in a retrieval system, or transmitted in any way by any means – electronic, mechanical, photocopy, recording, or otherwise, without the prior permission of the copyright holder, except as provided by USA copyright law.

Glory Wind Beneath My Wings: Copyright © 2010 by Regina G. Mixon
Printed in the United States of America

Bio's printed from author's websites with written permission

To God be the Glory!

To my daughter, *Emily Nicole Mixon.*
Thank you for your love and patience during
The many ups and downs we've faced.
As we journeyed together,
Your love, support, and understanding, gave me the strength
to keep going when I wanted to quit.
I love you.

❧ Introduction ❧

For every success story there are many people behind the scenes that help the visionary attain the vision. This book chronicles some of the ones that have been instrumental in my success as an author, speaker, publisher, mother, and person as a whole. These are unsung heroes that have been *The Wind Beneath My Wings*.

It is important for me to recognize these people and also to acknowledge the roles they played in the building of my ministries. This gives you a bit of background information about each person. These are and continue to be my heroes.

You, as a reader, probably have many people you would like to acknowledge for helping you attain your goals. I encourage you to take the opportunity to do so in whatever way God allows you to, as many don't realize how significant they have been in helping others. People do need to know.

In the words of Pastor Marvin Sapp, "I never would have made it and never could have made it" without each of those chronicled in this book. Read on and you will see that these people come from all walks of life—from students to professionals; from unemployed to incarcerated; from preachers and teachers to government employees—everyday people.

To God be the Glory!

To my daughter, *Emily Nicole Mixon.*
Thank you for your love and patience during
The many ups and downs we've faced.
As we journeyed together,
Your love, support, and understanding, gave me the strength
to keep going when I wanted to quit.
I love you.

Introduction

For every success story there are many people behind the scenes that help the visionary attain the vision. This book chronicles some of the ones that have been instrumental in my success as an author, speaker, publisher, mother, and person as a whole. These are unsung heroes that have been *The Wind Beneath My Wings*.

It is important for me to recognize these people and also to acknowledge the roles they played in the building of my ministries. This gives you a bit of background information about each person. These are and continue to be my heroes.

You, as a reader, probably have many people you would like to acknowledge for helping you attain your goals. I encourage you to take the opportunity to do so in whatever way God allows you to, as many don't realize how significant they have been in helping others. People do need to know.

In the words of Pastor Marvin Sapp, "I never would have made it and never could have made it" without each of those chronicled in this book. Read on and you will see that these people come from all walks of life—from students to professionals; from unemployed to incarcerated; from preachers and teachers to government employees—everyday people.

There are some that are retired, some that by the world's definition may not be of much value, some that profess to be Christians and some that do not. The one thing each has in common is at one point during my lifetime each believed in me and what I was doing and assisted in whatever way they could. Yes, they are my heroes and I thank God for each and every one of them.

As Paul said, not to say that I have arrived (far from it), but I have learned in whatsoever state I am in therewith to be content. It's only because I know beyond a shadow of a doubt that I have my heroes and she-roes in my life. And if the Lord never does anything else for me, He's done enough. He gave me people who love, appreciate, assist, and respect me in spite of me. And I, in turn, do the same for them. I'm blessed! We are blessed!

The writing of this book gives credit to those that I have drawn strength from over the years, those that are truly my heroes. I write this as a means of allowing you to briefly read and get to know the greatness in these knowing that each of you have your own unsung heroes.

Their acts of kindness were not performed for accolades, acknowledgement, or fanfare; but merely because of their belief in me as well as the desire to help me grow and accomplish my goals, visions, and dreams.

None profiled asked to be included in these writings. I never coaxed, or had to coax them into assisting me; I merely asked or told of my desire and they answered the call.

There is a saying that behind every great man there is a great woman. I believe that to be true; but behind every great woman usually there are many pushing and assisting in whatever way they can to help her become the best she can be. Prayers, assistance, words of encouragement, all were given and for this I say "thank you."

This book is a collaborative effort of the author and those profiled. Biographies' and pictures have been printed with the consent of those included in these writings.

Contents

Acknowledgement..................2
Introduction.........................3

Part 1: The Biological Family   7

Part 2: The Mentors/Teachers   15

Part 3: The Preachers/Pastors/Ministers   30

Part 4: The Social Security Administration   46

Part 5: The Sisters   50
Women of Purpose and Determination
Sisters of the Word/Meme Kelly
Black Women's Network
EnJoy Promotions/The 411 Café
A Meeting of the Minds Networking Group

Part 6: The Girlfriends   93

Part 7: The Brothers/Male Friends   104

Part 8: My Dream Team/REGS Books   123

Part 9: Conclusion   150

Part 1
The Formative Years/Biological Family

The Biological Family
The Foundation

Family is and has been extremely important and supportive for my entire life. Having a powerful, anointed, praying grandmother laid the foundation not only me but for our entire family. The most valuable principle she instilled in us was the love of God and the love of family. Yes, the foundation was laid from the very beginning.

I do not mention my mother much as she passed away when I was young. My memories of her are somewhat shady. The one thing I do remember is she, like my grandmother, her mother, loved and supported family.

Of my mother's children I have three siblings: Kelvin Mixon, Bruce Mixon and Dwayne Mixon. My father was married a few times and as a result of these marriages there were several other siblings: Dorothy Mozeke, Dock Mixon, Bobby Ray Taylor and Sonja Mixon.

Growing up in the house with my mother's children was an adventure. Like most siblings, we played, fought, laughed, cried, studied and learned together. And adding to those already mentioned, cousins: Mack Henry Richardson, Janet Elaine Richardson Brown-Jones, Dierdre Richardson, Shannon Richardson, Frenzella Richardson and Clifton Richardson were right along with us in most all that we did. I dare not fail to mention that we prayed together as a family; we went to church together as a family, and we worked together as a family.

We also had a few other cousins that we saw often as children even though they lived in Texas. We made frequent visits to and from Houston visiting Ronnie, Kenneth and Vincent Boyd along with their mother, my aunt now gone to be with the Lord, Minerva Boyd.

Aunt Minerva, until the year she died, would call me each year on my birthday to tell me how special I was and that she suggested the named Regina to my parents as Regina means queen. She always made me feel special. She made us all feel special.

Growing up in my grandmother's or mama's household was a time of much learning and much love. We quilted, along with my aunt Bertha Mitchell and my great-aunt, Beatrice Bell. We picked pecans, peas, corn and all kinds of fruits and vegetables.

Together with fig trees in the yard, were apple, peach and plum trees too. Mama had a garden that she proudly cultivated, raising greens, squash and a few other vegetables.

She taught us how to cook and clean. She taught us so much.

Family gatherings happened not just during the holiday season but all throughout the year. Back then, people would drop in at any time and the welcome mat, although not actually present, was seen by all. Everyone felt and knew they were welcomed when they set foot on those grounds.

We suffered losses throughout the years as slowly some started transitioning from this place to be with the Lord. Those were the hardest times for me.

My aunt Bertha stepped in when my mother died and became somewhat of a surrogate mother. Actually she was a cross between mother, best friend, big sister, aunt, counselor, and motivator, and she still is to this day. When ever I need to go to someone I know I can trust I run to her. She is always going to give me sound practical advice on how to deal with whatever I am going through. Priceless!

Janet is her daughter. She and I were raised more like sisters. Many people thought we were.

As we progressed in age, had children, got married and relocated, we continued to stay within immediate reach of each other. We babysat each others' children often rotating weekends. We were sisters.

During the time that I was brought up, whippings were still in style. There was no such thing as physical abuse and calling 911. Quite the opposite! It seems during that time when one misbehaved, everyone had a right to discipline the offender. They just knew how far to go. Neighbors, teachers, and friends' parents all had a right to put us in check, and by the time we got home we were disciplined again.

My brothers and I have always been extremely close. They let me know throughout the years they have always had my back. Kelvin and Bruce especially would jump in and fight anybody that tried to mess with their sister. They were and continue to be so protective. That's love!

Dwayne shows his love in a different way. He's not the one to jump in there because I've probably said something that I shouldn't have nor done something totally ridiculous. No, he's the one who supports and encourages me to no end to follow my passion and to do what is right. He and I, when we talk, actually talk for the longest time, usually sharing the goodness of God. Well Kelvin, Bruce and I do that too.

My brother, Bobby Ray, is another one who would immediately come to my rescue. If we were out somewhere and I happened to be at the same place as him, he would make it known in no uncertain terms that I was his sister and no one had better disrespect me-- another protective one.

Actually the majority of the men in my family—brothers, cousins, uncles—all have been very protective and supportive throughout my life. Yes, whenever I say I am going to people I know can be trusted usually those people are my biological family.

I moved to Los Angeles in 1989 staying until I returned to Louisiana in 1994. I then moved back to Los Angeles in September 2003 where I still reside. A few years prior to moving to Los Angeles in 1989 was when I really got to know my sister, Dorothy Mozeke. She is my sister by my father's first wife. I had met her before and knew of her but didn't really know her. She welcomed and embraced me and mine into her household and her family.

Dorothy has been nothing but the absolute best sister one could ask for. She, like the brothers, can be very protective. She's also very loving and kind and such a giving person. She will give someone the shirt off her back and as far as feeding the hungry—well all I can say is no one leaves her house hungry, ever! And none will go naked, not if she has anything or a dime to purchase something for someone.

Jeffery, her son, is yet another giving person. His daughter, Shyeta, is the same.

My cousins: Willie Gene Richardson, Mack Henry Richardson, Katherine Mixon, Mary Mixon, Odessa Taylor, Charles Mixon, and Shirley Mixon; uncle, Willie T. Richardson; sister-in-laws: Della Mixon, Phyllis Mixon, Ellen Gaines, Nellie Gaines, Brenda Arline, Shirley Arline Carter; brother-in-laws: Robert Arline Jr., Curtis Arline, Archie Arline , Joseph Gaines and Walter Thomas—to each of you I say "Thank you".

Della, Phyllis and I have had long- running relationships for many moons. My brothers did well in selecting their spouses. They are the best!

I was blessed to have two wonderful mothers-in-laws: Bertha Gaines and Mrs. Annie Arline (deceased).

To my nieces: Onekia Mixon, Shyeta Mozeke, Phylicia Mixon, and my nephews: Ladarrian Mixon, Dwayne Mixon II, and Jeffery Mozeke, I say "Thank you".

To my special cousins and god-children: Shiemetre Brown Smith, Kinedia Brown and April Brown, I give my heartfelt thanks for all you've done and continue to do.

To my daughter-in-law, Keisha Thomas, I thank God for having placed you in my family. You are the best daughter-in-law one could ever ask for.

Over the past year, I came to know other nieces and nephews: LaTretta White, Jenetta Johnson, Valerie Mixon, Rhonda Mixon and Jason Mixon. What a joy that has been! There are yet others that I have not met and do not know. I look forward to making the connections.

I've provided this information just for historical purposes. I want the world to know just how special these people are. There are so many others within my immediate family that I could list that have been instrumental in my success as a whole. There's not enough room to list them all. I could not, dare not exclude these three who have been around for as long as I can remember. Although not biological family, they are just as much family as the others. They are Willie James Bradford, Georgia Kirts and Willie Mae Calloway. They've been with us through thick and thin.

Trust is something earned after one proves themselves. I can honestly say my family members have proven themselves over and over again in my life. Yes, we are family and like many families we have our falling-outs from time to time. We've made many mistakes individually and collectively. We've missed the mark so many times but nevertheless, we are family and we stand together united in our love for God, our love for ourselves, our love for each other and our love for others. Yes, we are family and my family has been the backbone of my success as a person in general.

When I pursued a vision of mine of starting a ministry some years ago and fell, it was family who picked me up (after they talked about me ☺), provided me with temporary housing, purchased things my daughter and son needed and stood with me when the rest of the people walked away.

My biological family encouraged me, after they understood what I was attempting to do, assisted me spiritually, physically and financially, defended me, and stood by me.

Yes, my biological family is, and forever has been my backbone helping to shape me into the person I am today. They are and forever will be my heroes and the true wind beneath my wings.

God truly smiled on me and blessed me with what I consider to be the best family in the world. Never once in my lifetime have any of my family members told me or anyone else for that matter, that I would never amount to anything. Never once did any of my family members say that I had messed up so bad that I could not get back up, never once and the reason is because we are a family of visionaries. We are a family of "can do" people. We are a family of Bible believers. We are family! *Glory, the wind beneath my wings!*

Part 2
The Mentors/Teachers

As iron sharpens iron, so a friend sharpens a friend.
Proverbs 27:17

Frankie Mitchell
Retired Educator

From her lips to yours, "To write about myself is to express my love for God, the Father; Jesus, the Son and the Holy Spirit. This love can be shared with others as we live from day to day. I want to make a difference as I pass this way. If I can help somebody, Lord, please let it be."

Frankie L. Wilson Mitchell, born June 14, 1935 to the late Luther and Rotena Carter Wilson was one of eight children.

Because her parents were interested in them receiving a good education, all of the children finished Webster High School and all but three finished college.

Mrs. Wilson attended Southern University, Baton Rouge and graduated with a major in English and a minor in Literary Science.

She and Harvey Mitchell Jr. married December 24, 1958 and had two children—Michael and Hazel.

After teaching for 25 years, in 1994 she announced her intentions to seek a seat on the Webster Parish School

Board and ultimately won. She has since been re-elected four times unopposed.

Because of her genuine love for people—rich, poor, black, white, drop-outs, graduates, etc., she loves to help in any way as you will witness yourself from these writings.

With all of her accomplishments and involvements, she remains humble; and is never too busy or involved to find time to reverence God.

Mrs. Mitchell was honored in the third edition of *Who's Who Among America's Teachers,* 1994 having been selected by former students. Students were requested to nominate teachers who made a difference in their lives by helping to shape their values, inspire interest in a particular subject and/or challenge them to strive for excellence.

One student wrote about Mrs. Mitchell, "She made education something pleasurable, instead of a dreadful ordeal, by letting me spread my wings and showing me the best way to fly." During the time of this nomination Mrs. Mitchell was teaching at Minden High School, Minden Louisiana.

Mrs. Mitchell received special thanks from the Webster Junior High School National Beta Club where the Principal is Elena Black. They said and I quote," Because of you, our Beta Club had another successful year. Thank you for your continued interest in our educational endeavors as well as our service to the community."

Mrs. Mitchell is a member of the Mt. Calm Baptist Church in Minden, Louisiana where the Rev. T. Alexander Knapp serves as her pastor.

She is also a member of the Delta Sigma Theta Sorority for more than fifty years, a member of the Martin Luther King Committee and a member of the NAACP.

Other involvements include—
- Member of the Webster Parish Finance Committee
- Chairman Curriculum Committee
- Member Long Range Study Committee
- Louisiana School Board Association Board of Directors representing District 5
- Louisiana State Legislative Committee
- Louisiana State Testing Committee
- Past Member LSBA Scholarship Committee
- Past Member LSBA Resolution Committee
- Recipient of a Certificate Award for Distinguished Service presented by the National School Board Association in recognition of an unparalleled commitment to America's children through school board leadership and service
- NSBA Federal Relations Network attendee
- LSBA Delegate
- LSBA Regional attendee

I echo the sentiments of those students that nominated Mrs. Mitchell for inclusion in *Who's Who Among America's Teachers.* Mrs. Mitchell inspired me at an early age and made me believe that nothing was impossible—no goal, vision or dream.

Many don't realize how acts of kindness and words of encouragement can have a lifelong affect on the recipient. Knowing that someone believes in you, I mean really believes in you, is priceless and an investment that may possibly yield many rewards later.

When I had my first child, dropped out of high school, went to Adult Education classes and took the GED early, Mrs. Mitchell was my biggest cheerleader.

Having taken the test about three years before my class graduated, I was assured by the school board that my scores would be kept until my class graduated and I would be allowed to receive my diploma at that time. The time rolled around to 1975, the year my class would graduate, and the scores had been lost. Feeling a little downhearted, Mrs. Mitchell said to me, "Come on Mixon and take the test again. You can do it."

Well, I took it for the second and final time and yes, I passed the test. She just could not leave it alone. She was so proud. I remember her words like it was yesterday. "Mixon, you know what? I believe you scored higher this time around. I knew you could do it." Talk about a lasting impression.

Mrs. Mitchell has always been down to earth, loves the Lord, and so easy to talk to. And she does make time for anyone. She truly loves people.

At our ten year class reunion she was the speaker. She issued a challenge to our class to become investors. She stated at that time that if we invested a certain amount she would match it. We didn't take her up on the offer but once again she was our cheerleader, our encourager, our supporter, our "can do" person and that has stuck with me for a lifetime.

Excellent. Real. Friendly. Loving. Supportive. Family-oriented. Anointed. Helpful. Pleasant. The list goes on and on but suffice it to say that Mrs. Frankie L. Wilson Mitchell is and forever will be my hero.

It pleases me so to give honor to whom honor is due and tribute to whom tribute is due in the person of Mrs. Frankie L. Wilson Mitchell.

Mrs. Mitchell, did you ever know that you were my hero? I can fly higher than an eagle because you are the wind beneath my wings!

I have committed my life to *paying it forward* and I will share with every one I come in contact with the positive effect you have had in my life.

Jewel Diamond Taylor

www.donotgiveup.net

Speaker-Minister-Author- Life Coach-Workplace Training- Retreat Facilitator

Jewel Diamond Taylor aka "The Self Esteem Dr." is a native of Washington, D. C. She is married to John Taylor with two adult sons. Her church home is Imani Christian Temple in Pomona, CA. where her pastor is Bishop Elect Jelani F. Kafela.

Jewel is the author of several books: *"Sisterfriends"," You Deserve More: Desperation is a Terrible Perfume to Wear", "Success Gems", "You Are Too Blessed to be*

Stressed", "The Main Thing is to KEEP the Main Thing the Main Thing" and author of the popular black history poem written in 1987 "I'm Not Giving My Black Back" included in her *"Sisterfriends"* book.

Jewel served as my mentor for approximately two years. Under her guidance and direction, I have grown as a speaker, a business-person and an author; I have grown as a person.

Jewel is a licensed minister serving at her church. She ministers to the masses throughout the United States and other parts of the world, encouraging, motivating, inspiring and educating her audiences.

Jewel has numerous teaching tapes and regularly does one-on-one mentoring sessions with individuals encouraging and assisting them to go and grow.

Jewel is the founder of Women on the Grow, Super Goal Saturday Motivational Seminars, the Don't Give Up Conferences and Women's Paragon Leadership Training Series.

Jewel, I thank God for placing you in my life during the season I needed your help the most. I value our friendship and consider you not only a hero of mine, but one to many.

Dr. Netreia D. Carroll
www.netreiadcarrollministries.com
Publisher–Pastor–Author–Humanitarian

Angels are ethereal, celestial beings with wings, in the likeness of humans but thought to be superior to them, sent by God to guard and guide us. This is the image usually envisioned when one mentions angels. Some angels are unknown to us; others we assume to know, hence the phrase "You are such an angel." Of course, one must have certain attributes to qualify as an angel. According to Webster (not to sound cliché), an angel generally possesses attributes of beauty, purity or kindliness. Dr. Carroll aka Mother Theresa, San Diego, a multidimensional, talented and incredible humanitarian, truly exemplifies those qualities.

Dr. Carroll's life was struck with tragedy at a young age. She was six months old when the Lord took her mother home to be with Him. Her loving godparents stepped in and helped to raise her in Riverside, California for the first few years of her life. Then her father remarried and brought her home to San Diego to be with him. Now a part of a blended family, with two brothers and two sisters, she seems unscathed by her earlier ill-fated life experience.

"Singing is my first gift and acting came later," said Dr. Carroll, who started her vocal endeavors at age seven and her acting in the sixth grade. She never went to parties, not even "Grad Night," and rarely hung out with her peers. "And I never smoked or drank", Dr. Carroll adds. Instead, she stayed focused on her love for singing, opting to travel with her usually older cast members performing at various concerts throughout the United States. Now forty-four, Dr. Carroll continues to share her musical talent through theater, and at various Christian venues. Her credits include Tambourines to Glory, The Wiz, Cinderella Jones, When It Hits Home, Passion and Honey, Ceremonies in Dark Old Men, Standing in the Gap, Harlem Harlem, Come All Ye Faithful, to name a few.

Although a longtime member of Blessed Assurance Baptist Church, under the direction of Pastor Gregory A. Brown, Dr. Carroll believes that, just as Jesus taught the disciples by example and sent them out to minister, she was chosen to do the same. Beginning on Sunday mornings in December 2000, the salon/coffee shop she owned transformed into the newly established church named, "The Shabach House Ministries" derived from Shaback Inc., an already established ministry that Dr. Carroll founded. Shabach means to commend or to praise God and was approved by Jesus. Dr. Carroll began her education at Imani Kuumba Christian College, then to Logos Christian University of Florida entering their (masters program) and completed receiving her doctoral degree in religious arts and Biblical studies with life experience combined from Suffield University, an international, non-traditional university. Her education is recognized by the National Distance Learning Association International. She also holds a Bachelors in Science.

Dr. Carroll is the author of "Satan Get Out of My House", a book that deals with the family and can be found in any online book store. Dr. Carroll says, "Satan comes to destroy the family. He comes in full force, and never lightly. In this book, you will find biblical principles as God instructs us on how to prepare ourselves as we are faced with the enemy's undersized dilemmas. Don't allow Satan to destroy your family or your home. Kick him out!"

GOAL: Let love do the drawing.
MISSION: Embracing authors worldwide through LOVE and not through MONEY.
KINGDOM PURPOSE: Serving the sick, poor, needy and burying the dead according to the Word of God.

Dr. Carroll published my first book through her publishing company: Affordable Publishing. She has served as my mentor in book publishing and also designed book covers for my books.

Dr. Carroll opened the door for my very first speaking engagement at a *Breaking Free Conference* held in San Diego, California. She is a real trooper, one who lives by example, and one I am proud to know.

Read Dr. Carroll's full biography on her website: www.shaback.net. or www.netreiadcarrollministries.com

DeBorah B. Pryor
Journalist–Public Speaker–Actor

A Theatre and Psychology major at San Francisco State University, **DeBorah B. Pryor** is a respected journalist and passionate public speaker and conversationalist with more than 30-years experience in the field of communications. She has worked extensively in the corporate, private and nonprofit sectors; in public relations at New York's acclaimed **Metropolitan Opera Company**; as personal assistant to music icon **Sly Stone**; as a Job Search Counselor at **The Urban League** in Northern California; in Sales at the former **92.3 The Beat** radio in Los Angeles; in the area of special needs as both executive assistant and executive director.

A former stage actor and radio host, DeBorah's extensive communications career has taken her around the globe. In 2001 she accompanied Martin Luther King III, Chuck D. and others to Dominica, West Indies by invitation of former Prime Minister, Roosie Douglas; and her work in journalism has net her more than 400 published articles;

and personal interviews with some of the world's most celebrated people from entertainment, politics and literature. She is the founder of *Public Speaking for the Private Person*, an original 4-hour training program she designed to arm professionals from all walks of life with great "on-the-job" public speaking abilities and strategies that will enable their confidence, initiative, skill and assertiveness in their various professions. This incredible seminar has recently become a 2-disc CD.

Currently featured in the Inaugural Edition of *Who's Who in Black Los Angeles,* DeBorah is the proud mother of Azja, a former casting assistant with Paramount; and the creator of the high-end greeting cards under *Lily & Company*. She is grandmother to Destin; the globetrotting young son of actor **Chris Tucker**. DeBorah is a one-third partner in the Los Angeles-based public relations firm **The Bio Shop**. Her website is available at www.dpryorpresents.com

And he gave some, apostles; and some, prophets; and some, evangelists; and some, pastors and teachers; for the perfecting of the saints, for the work of the ministry, for the edifying of the body of Christ. Ephesians 4:11-12

Part 3
The Pastor's/Preachers/Ministers

Rev. Robert J. White
Preacher–Truck Driver

Rev. Robert J. White is a minister who attends Greater Hope Baptist Church in Shreveport, Louisiana under the leadership of Pastor Wilber Dawson. He is a truck driver and also ministers the word of God to many encouraging them to accept Christ and live for him.

When not ministering the word or driving trucks, Rev. White enjoys walking and exercising, playing dominoes, reading and studying the Bible. His favorite scriptures come from John 14 and Proverbs 3:3-5.

Rev. White has seven siblings, most of which are in the southern states.

Rev. Robert White helped me and mine when we could not help ourselves. While pursuing involvement in the ministry God's Storehouse in Louisiana, it was his generosity that provided us housing.

Not only did he provide housing, his purchase of the house previously owned by myself, afforded us the opportunity to assist many in need providing a home-based business.

Information & Referral Services, food distribution, and donations of furniture, dishes, pots, pans and the like to those in need were provided from this residence.

The original plan was that he would purchase the house to provide me with funds to pay bills and pursue the ministry and I, after obtaining operating capital that would include a salary for me, would regain the property. Things did not work as planned. As a result of this, Rev. White ended up losing the house due circumstances beyond our control.

Even though there were some times my family and I occasionally had to live with various family members due to lack of finances, his act of kindness afforded me the opportunity to pursue my dream, and as a result help many even when my family and I were in need. For this I am eternally grateful thanking God that he was there when I needed him.

Pastor Rodney Williams
Pastor, King Solomon Baptist Church
Sibley, LA

Rodney E. Williams is a pastor, musician and two time author. He has been a music minister for twenty- five years. His many gifts have allowed him to frequent many different settings and cities. This gift of preaching, playing, and singing has carried him across many denominational lines as well. It is through this work that Pastor Williams desires to spark an interest in the hearts of every church member, musician, worship leader and pastor to "Reach For The Praise." Pastor Williams resides in Sibley, Louisiana with his wife Cynthia and their children. He presently serves as pastor of the King Solomon Baptist Church.

Pastor Williams is the author of two books, *"Gone by Faith"* and *"Reach for the Praise"*

Pastor Williams served as my pastor for a short while. During this time, he and his wife reached out to help me in ways that none had ever done before. He helped restore my belief that there are good, God-fearing people with a desire to help others in a time of need.

Pastor W. Terrell Snead, II
Senior Pastor, Kingdom Builders Fellowship, Long Beach, CA
www.kbfellowship.org

Pastor Snead, II was born on January 28, 1967. He is married to CaSaundra D. Snead and is the father of two daughters and two sons.

Pastor Snead, II graduated from Long Beach Polytechnic High School; studied business administration at Long Beach City College; took classes in religious studies at Los Angeles Bible College; attended Macedonia International Bible Fellowship, School of Pastoral Ministry and Long Beach Bible College.

Pastor Snead accepted his call to preach the gospel and was licensed in 1992 and ordained in 1998.

He has served as the assistant to the pastor at the Greater Temple of God Missionary Baptist Church of Los Angeles, California, under the leadership of Dr. W. T. Snead, Sr.

Under the leadership of the late Bishop James E. Henry, Pastor Snead, II served as the Assistant Pastor of the Victory Bible Full Gospel Baptist Church of Pasadena, California. Following God's call, Pastor Snead, II organized and served as Pastor at the New Beginning Bible Fellowship Church of Altadena, California.

In 2004, Pastor W. Terrell Snead, II was called to serve as Senior Pastor of The Word of God Missionary Baptist Church of Los Angeles, California. Under Pastor Snead's leadership, membership grew spiritually and numerically, The Symbol of Hope Community Development Corporation was established and The Word of God Outreach Ministry has grown to feed and clothe the hungry, needy and homeless. Pastor Snead also organized WTS 2 Ministries, and in March 2007 he established the "MySpace/His Space Conference," a vehicle designed to teach a generation about internet integrity, and to challenge them to raise their morals and values in life.

In October 2008, Pastor Snead being led by the Holy Spirit organized a group of believers for Bible study and on the first Sunday in December 2008 Kingdom Builders Fellowship was birthed. This church is committed to building the Kingdom of God and equipping the body of Christ in Kingdom living.

Pastor Snead's approach to ministry and leading God's church is based on Ephesians 4:11, 12. He says his gifting and calling is to lead God's people to become D.E.E.P. in the things of God. D.E.E.P. represents Discipling, Equipping, Evangelizing and Praying. He believes that this is the formula that God has given him to lead His church to the next level.

Pastor Snead and his family touched my family's life in a powerful way. The entire family is involved in ministry yet they are as down to earth as can be.

They do not profess to be perfect and share various trials and struggles they've gone through as a means of encouraging others.

They have sown seeds of the Word into my life that prayerfully will produce a great harvest.

During some of the most challenging and difficult times in my life, they were there— not being critical or judgmental, but supportive. They offered words of encouragement and assistance in whatever way they could.

Our children became friends. We became friends. We became something bigger and better than just friends—we became family.

I reflect on his teachings from a while ago. He announced to the congregation, "Well people I have some news for you today. The good news is we are family. The bad news is we are family."

Families go through so much together: praying, playing, working, learning, growing AND the inevitable falling outs, but in spite of it all, when the rubber meets the road, family is there. Thank God for family.

Upon further reflections, I said that people when faced with difficulties go to who they know can be trusted. Don't get me wrong, family can and often will let each other down, but the good news is that those in the body of Christ understand that family will also stand with you and fight for you and even dare anyone to say a negative thing about the other.

Yes, they've proven themselves to me and mine and for this I can only say thank you.

Pastor Snead, Sister Snead and the entire Snead family, be blessed. Let me encourage you. Let me speak life to you. You can depend on God to see you through and you can definitely depend on me to keep you covered in prayer as you embark upon your new journey. I thank God for each of you.

Mighty, powerful, anointed, humble family!

Pastor Ron C. Hill
Pastor, Love & Unity Christian Fellowship
Compton, California
www.loveandunity.org

The youngest of four children, Pastor Ronald C. Hill was raised in the small town of Pittsburg, Texas. When he was eight years old he accepted Jesus Christ into his life but experienced little spiritual growth. After graduating from high school, he joined the United States Navy and completed two tours of duty in Vietnam. In 1967, he was honorably discharged and moved to Los Angeles, California where he worked in the aircraft industry. The following year, he accepted a job with the Southern California Transit District.

In 1972 Pastor Hill rededicated his life to God. Shortly thereafter, the Lord instructed him to quit his job and go into ministry full time. A year later, the Lord opened a door for Pastor Hill to become the first African American minister to serve as chaplain with the Union Rescue Mission in Los Angeles. From 1973 to 1980, Pastor Hill also served as an evangelist and chaplain with the Los Angeles County Probation Department. In 1981, Pastor Ronald C. Hill founded the Love and Unity Church of God in Christ in the city of Compton, California. The ministry began with Pastor Hill, his wife, their four small children and a few church members and has now grown to over 3,500 members. As of September 2009, the church transitioned and became Love and Unity Christian Fellowship. Pastor Hill is strongly committed to the mission of spreading the good news and winning souls for Christ and teaching the body of Christ's biblical principles they can apply to their everyday lives.

Pastor Ronald C. Hill has been married to Evangelist, Missionary Osie L. Hill for thirty-nine years. God has blessed them with four children: Angela, Constance, Ronald Jr., and Joseph.

Pastor Ronald C. Hill hosts a daily radio broadcast, "Food for Your Soul Morning Show" on KTYM Radio (1460 AM Inglewood CA) and is a regular guest speaker on Trinity Broadcasting Network.

Pastor Hill currently serves as my pastor. He and Lady Osie embraced me shortly after I joined the church and even had me as a guest on their radio broadcast. He has asked me when I will use my gifts and talents in *that* church. Even though I've skirted the issue the time is rapidly approaching.

They are ever the encouragers, giving the unadulterated word of God using real life's experiences to drive the message home, while loving the congregants and community as a whole.

Pastor and the Love & Unity Christian Fellowship, feed the hungry on a regular basis, clothe the naked, visits those in prison, and are out and about in the highways and byways telling of God's goodness—it's called walking the walk that Jesus walked.

Pastor said some time ago that he wanted people to know his heart. He asked people to pray for God to show us his heart. I heeded his request and God answered the prayer. He showed me that this man is a man after His own heart and desires nothing more than to serve Him to the fullest.

Leading by example; he and his entire family work together in the ministry. They truly show that families can and should pray together, work together, play together, grow together and prosper together.

Even though I've still shacked—having the benefit of a relationship without being fully committed—they still embrace, encourage and accept me as one of their own. For this, I am eternally grateful.

To those that may misconstrue the term shacking mentioned above, this does not refer to my living with anyone or engaging in conduct inappropriate as a Christian. In *Pursuing Your Purpose with Passion* I gave my definition of shacking. It bears repeating. Shacking is anytime one is not fully committed to the relationship and not utilizing their time, talents, gifts and resources to fully support the partnership. Yes, I've been a bit slothful as it relates to the church. Now that that's cleared up, Pastor and

Sister Osie, I love you both with the love of God—unconditionally.

Pastor Charlie Winzer
Pastor, Agape New Beginnings Ministries
Minden, Louisiana

Of all the pastors mentioned in these writings, Pastor Winzer was the one who served as my pastor for the longest period of time. Our relationship began in the 1980's when he became my pastor at Rocky Mount Baptist Church in the rural area of Claiborne Parish. Not only was I a member there but several of my family members were as well. I stayed until 1989 when I relocated to California.

Upon leaving California in 1994 and returning to Louisiana, I found that Pastor Winzer was now pastoring New Light Baptist Church in Minden, Louisiana and joined there. His teachings throughout the years helped shape my beliefs as a person and as a Christian.

Pastor Winzer allowed me to use my gifts and talents, as he did with all other members, for God's glory. God used him to help lay a solid foundation in my life through the Word of God.

One piece of advice he gave me that I live by to this day is "Whenever you can rise above what others say and think and be obedient to the Holy Spirit is when God can really use you". Well Pastor Winzer, God can really use me now.

Rev. Victor Carter
Minister of Music–Funeral Director

Rev. Victor Carter has always and forever been my hero. You see, we are family—not blood related but related through the marriage between his aunt and my uncle. We are and have been family in the truest sense for many years.

Rev. Carter served as Minister of Music during my time at New Light Baptist Church. I have been many places and I can truly say under his guidance and direction any choir he directs and presides over is awesome. The anointing of God falls heavily on him like a cloak. His is for real.

Rev. Carter also is employed with Benevolent Funeral Home in Minden. Married to Shryl Carter, they are the parents of two children: Zaccheus and Emmanuel.

In addition to his employment with Benevolent Funeral Home, he currently serves as Minister of Music for both New Light Baptist Church and Agape New Beginnings Ministries.

> Synergy: The sum of all of us is greater than any of us individually.

Part 4
The Social Security Administration Family

Social Security Administration
Torrance, CA

Joining the Social Security family many years ago was one of the best things that ever happened for me. Having had the opportunity to work in several different offices, I found that there is such a bond developed and we are family in every sense of the word.

Social Security ranked number six in 2010 as one of the top ten places to work in the government.

The employees, contrary to some beliefs, are genuinely caring and committed individuals, concerned about each person served. These are dedicated individuals with a heart for the people and a desire to serve.

Pictured above is the staff of the Torrance, California Social Security Office. However I've had the privilege of working in Social Security Offices in Minden, Louisiana; Inglewood, California; Los Angeles, California; and the

Crenshaw Social Security Office. I've found the qualities and characteristics of the employees to be the same in each office.

Those I've worked with have been and still are family, friends, and mentors. Many have become lifelong friends. Some have just been in my life for a season. Regardless of the season and/or the reason, I thank God for having the opportunity to work for and with some of the best people in the world.

The Minden, Louisiana office is not pictured; however, this was where my career began. Having met the likes of Pam Brunson, Gloria Matthews Alstork, Emma Matthews, Sandra Wafer, Howard Doughty, Janice Austin, Sybil Ray, Linda Murphy, James Stephens, Ted Robinson, Joe Heard, Christine McDonald (deceased), Debra Miller-Mills, Irv Baggett, Bonnie Woodfork (deceased), Mary Abercrombie, and so many more, and working with them, I knew that this was the career path I wanted to pursue. Their adoption of me into their family (or mine of them depending on who came first) made the decision an easy one.

I say thank you to each of you. Your acts of kindness and love have helped shape and create me into the person I am today—a person with a true heart to serve.

I dare not close this out without mentioning Margaret Knight, Stephanie Taylor, John Steiner, Donna Barlow-Oglesby, Barbara Haynes, Tiffany Wilson, Tex Matthews and Glen Banks. Each of these also offered much help in various ways, and for this I can only say thank you.

I would love to mention names of some individually in the Torrance office but have been told in no uncertain terms to not do so. You know who you are. I love you all.

Again, I thank those mentioned and give God the glory for allowing me to do what I love with people I have grown to respect, admire, appreciate, and love.

Part 5
The Sisters

Women of Purpose and Determination
EnJoy Promotions/The 411 Network
Sisters of the Word Book Club
Black Women's Network
Meeting of the Minds Networking Group

Women of Purpose and Determination
Minden, LA

(Pictured above Annette Jones Davidson, Beverly Kennon Thornton, Audrey Reed Flournoy, Rose Thornton Kinsey, Cynthia Lewis Combs, Jackie Lewis Rice, Marzetta Wright Murray and Gloria Combs Morris. Not pictured Jacqueline Graham Chapman, Angela Wills, Germaine Turk, Regina Mixon and Barbara Johnson Smith)

Women of Purpose and Determination's Creed

I am a Woman of Purpose and Determination.

I am more than a conqueror in Christ Jesus.

I will pursue my purpose with passion and determination.

I will always place God first in my life and seek Him for guidance.

I walk by faith and not by sight.

I serve God by serving others.

I will use my gifts and talents to serve others.

I am a member of a team.

I will help lift my sister up if she falls.

I will always try to breed peace and unity among others.

I am an expert and I am a professional.

I will continually grow in all areas of my life.

I will always cultivate a healthy mind, body, and spirit.

I am disciplined, spiritually, physically, and mentally tough, trained and stand ready to fight the good fight of faith.

I will never give up.

I am a Woman of Purpose and Determination.

Annette Jones-Davidson
Women of Purpose and Determination Founder
US Military Employee

A native of Minden, Louisiana, Annette has proven to be a very huge part of my success. We have known each other since elementary school and still love and support each other to this day. I consider her a true, loving, and caring friend.

She is a graduate of Minden High School and has earned a B.S. Degree in business administration from American Technological University in Lawton, OK. She is a conference hostess and workshop presenter. Annette has worked for the federal government for twenty-four years.

Annette currently resides in Columbia, SC. She loves to travel and has traveled to many countries, including Germany, France, Italy, Korea, England, Japan, and Holland. One of her goals is to visit every state in the U.S. At this time she has visited over half of them.

She attends Bibleway Church of Atlas Road. Her pastor is Elder Darrell Jackson.

Annette is the Founder and Director of the non-profit organization "Women of Purpose and Determination" (WOPD). The organization's mission is to encourage women to become the woman that they were created to be, and to develop and use their gifts and talents to help themselves and others. She returns to her hometown every year where the organization hosts their annual women's conference.

Anointed is a word that easily and quickly comes to mind when I think of Annette. Another word that comes to mind is *caring,* as she has a heart for people and a desire to help people first and foremost come to know God by developing a relationship with Him and secondly to be the best that they can be.

She is a natural motivator. Annette opened the door for me to speak at "Women of Purpose and Determination" events having never heard me speak; she had faith enough in God and me to believe that I could do—and, I had only spoken a couple of times prior to those events. She is a faith-filled, spirit-led woman.

Annette is the wife of James L. Davidson, also of Minden, LA. They have two grown children, Jamia and Christopher. They also have one grandchild, Tyler.

Rose Thornton Kinsey
Educator–Speaker–Women of Purpose & Determination Member

As an educator of the past twenty-five years, I have learned children are little people with the same needs as big people. I have spent most of my teaching career in Bossier City, Louisiana, and after I moved to Vicksburg, Mississippi, I came to the realization that all students need to be accepted, nurtured, disciplined, motivated, respected, and taught how to achieve academic and social excellence. I try to instill in my students more than just lessons in a book, but a deeper meaning for life itself: how to think, how to choose the right choices instead of the wrong. The most important lesson is that there are consequences for your behavior in life, positive and negatives.

However, you choose which consequence you want in your life. I have learned as a teacher, that the power of words is so vital to students. It is imperative that I speak life to those students that cross my path; encouragement goes a long ways with all students. I believe that each child has a unique story to tell; I learn from my students and they from me, and I'm learning to be a better listener. My philosophy is that every child can achieve success at something and children have interesting things to say that can enrich all of our lives in a positive way, if we take the time to listen and evaluate what they are saying.

Having come from a large family, I can say there was one sure surplus and that was love. My grandmother taught me that love for your fellow man was worth more than all the silver or gold or any material thing that money can buy. I have two brothers and four sisters. My siblings and I were taught how to love God, by the example of my grandmother who showed us her love for God through helping others in the community, attending prayer meetings, church, Sunday school and Bible study each week. She taught us the golden rule, respect for others and treating others the way you want to be treated. These values have been embedded in my mind and helped me to become a teacher.

I am a mother of two children: my older child Tamika Grant, who is a teacher as well in the Caddo Parish School System and my younger child Gary Jiles, Jr., who lives in Shreveport, Louisiana. Both of my children are married. I am blessed with a grandson, Richard Grant II, who is an A honor student at Justin Elementary School in Shreveport, Louisiana. I am married to Marlon T. Kinsey, who is a chemist for Shell Lubricant Plant in Vicksburg, Mississippi.

My professional development involves a commitment to continued growth in knowledge and skills, participating in numerous academic and social developments to help me acquire expertise in becoming a life long learner in education.

Education:
Earned a Bachelor of Science degree in elementary education at Grambling State University in Grambling, Louisiana (December 16, 1985)
Continued graduate studies: Louisiana State University, Shreveport, Louisiana (July 2005 - August 2005)
Louisiana Endowment for Humanities (LEH)
For the teaching of America history (received continued education points)

Mild Moderate Certification for Behavior Disordered Students (June 2000)
Louisiana Tech University, Ruston Louisiana
Hours toward a master's degree in supervision (June 2003)
University of Alabama, Tuscaloosa, Alabama (July 2005)
Science Summer Institute (research experience for middle and high school teachers).
Attended continuing education classes, workshops and conferences in Vicksburg, Mississippi to improve for self-growth and to continue learning and implementing the latest trends in education.

I have served on several committees and task forces against drugs and have taught drug and awareness classes for youth. I have also given speeches and presentation at the NAACP banquet, family reunions, community workshops, and churches. I am a proud member of WOPD (Women of Purpose and Determination), which focuses on serving and helping the community in a positive manner by lifting up the name of Jesus. We encourage others to be the best they can be always striving for excellence. We give food, clothing items, school supplies, and other support to the needy in Minden, Louisiana; we assist with the planning, organizing, implementing, and coordinating of awareness workshops and women's conferences. Our organization's headquarters is in Columbia, South Carolina. The awareness workshops and women's conferences are all held in Minden, Louisiana.

I have served as the president of the New Notes Choir, president of the Willing Workers, Sunday school teacher for pre-school and young adults, and as chairperson of numerous church plays and musicals. I have worked with the youth as a Vacation Bible School teacher, and assisted with youth on outings at the Mount Calm Baptist in

Minden, Louisiana. I am very committed in reaching out and providing a helping hand with great sincerity and devotion in up lifting the name of Jesus.

Serving as a youth speaker for a workshop in Vicksburg, Mississippi, at the Travel's Rest Baptist Church, I attend Travel's Rest Baptist Church in Vicksburg, Mississippi on a weekly basis to get spiritual wisdom and knowledge from God.

I am involved with giving food and clothing to the needy, and I have always been supportive of the March of Dimes and Families in Crisis. These organizations are located in Vicksburg, Mississippi. If there is ever a time to make the difference, it is now! It is important that we do our part in making our days here on earth count for something positive.

Below are a list of awards and recognition I have received doing my years of teaching:

Warren Central Intermediate Awarded Behavior Excellence 2008 – 2009
Vicksburg, Mississippi, Warren County School District
Warren Central Intermediate Awarded for Academic Improvement 2008 – 2009
Vicksburg, Mississippi, Warren County School District
Warren Central Intermediate Technology Committee
Vicksburg, Mississippi, Warren County School District 2008 – 2009
Warren Central Intermediate Awarded Behavior Excellence 2007 – 2008
Vicksburg, Mississippi, Warren County School District
Warren Central Intermediate Awarded for Academic Excellence   2006 – 2008

Vicksburg, Mississippi, Warren County School District
Warren Central Intermediate Black History Poster Contest
Winner   2008– 2009
Vicksburg, Mississippi, Warren County School District
Perfect Attendance Award Princeton Elementary
2006 – 2007
Certificate of Appreciation Princeton Elementary
2006 – 2007
Louisiana State University
Certificate of Completion Teaching American History
Institute   May 2006
Alabama State University
July 2006
Certificate of Completion Integrated Science
Certificate of Appreciation Charlotte
2005 – 2006
Teacher of the Year Charlotte Mitchell
2004 – 2005
Teacher of the Year Charlotte Mitchell
2003 –2004
Certificate of Excellence Charlotte Mitchell
October 2004
Renaissance Learning, Mathematics, Charlotte Mitchell
May 2004
Certificate of Excellence
Louisiana Federation of Teachers
Oct 2004
Life Skills Training Charlotte Mitchell
July 2002
Annual Career Day, Chairperson, Charlotte Mitchell
May 2003
Newspaper Coordinator, Charlotte Mitchell
Technology Louisiana INTECH, Charlotte Mitchell
2003 –2004

Path to Excellence   Charlotte
     2000
State Winner Poetry Contest Butler Elementary School
May 1998
Certificate Appreciation Butler Elementary School
May 1999
Regional Winner Poetry Contest Butler Elementary
May 1998
Career Day Award Butler Elementary School
May 1997
Jefferson Award Butler Elementary School
(Outstanding Teacher Award Recommend by Parents)
May 1997
Workshop Coordinator "I Believe I Can Fly"
(To Improve Math and Reading Scores)
April 1997
Nomination as "Teacher of the Year" Council
For Exceptional Children"
Jan   1994
Teacher of the Month Butler Elementary School
Jan   1991

I believe like the writer who stated:
One Hundred Years from now: One Hundred Years from now; It will not matter what kind of car I drove, What kind of house I lived in, how much money was in my bank account, nor what my clothes looked like. But the world may be a better place because I was important in the life of a child ((*excerpt from "Within My Power" by Forest Witcraft*).

Work Experience:
Princeton Elementary School, Haughton, Louisiana
 (August 2006 – May 2007)
Special Education Teacher (4th and 5th grades)

After School Tutoring - LEAP Test (tutoring lessons designed for grade 4, students for remediation Math)

Charlotte Ann Mitchell, Bossier, City, Louisiana (August 2002 – May 2006)
Regular Education Teacher (5th and 6th grades)
Organized and Implemented Alcohol Awareness Program
Developed and facilitated Career Day Programs
Facilitated Workshops

Southern University, Shreveport, Louisiana
Voyager Med Camp and Technology Camp (June 2003 – June 2004)
After school tutoring - working with at-risk students (August 2005)
Success InSite Program, Bossier City, Louisiana (May 2000 – 2005)
Counselor mental health rehabilitation clients
Parental and individual counseling for self-development
Organized and implemented behavior management plans clients and parents
Monitored and documented strengths and weaknesses for client and parents
Implemented social skills (role - played and used techniques to defuse poor anger control with students and parents)
Analyzed behavior results: evaluated and collect data

Butler Elementary School, Bossier City, Louisiana (May 1989 – August 2003)
Special Education Teacher (EBD) Emotional Behavior Disordered – 4th and 5th graders)
Lead Teacher – Special Education
School Improvement Committee

Analyzed and developed Individualized Educational Program for each student
Workshops for teachers and parents (I Believe I Can Fly Workshop)
Career Day coordinator
Annual Fall Carnival coordinator

Angela Wills
Recording Artist–Women of Purpose & Determination
Member–Teacher–Writer

This illustrious songstress, hailing from Minden, Louisiana, is the voice of the music to my book trailer for *"To God be the Glory"*. When called upon to sing the song for the trailer, she did not hesitate, and to my surprise wrote and recorded her own version of the song. It coincides beautifully with the message contained in the writings of the book.

The daughter of Minister Charles Wills and the late Bobbie Wills, Angela has three siblings: Darron Wills, Adrienne Wills and Andrea Jones. She is the mother of one son, Jacquari Wills.

Currently employed with Citifinancial, Angela's mission is one of uplifting and encouraging those in need.

As a child, I was at one time Angela's babysitter. Her parents and I were extremely close because I had worked with her mother many years ago. To my amazement, she grew up with the vocal skills of her mother and blossomed into a beautiful young woman.

Angela is a faithful member of the Mt. Calm Baptist Church of Minden, Louisiana under the leadership of Rev. T. Alexander Knapp, serving on the praise team, as a Sunday school teacher, an advisor to the youth choir, and president of what is currently Friendship Young Adult Ministry, and she can always be found singing praises unto God in the choir.

Angela is in the process of completing her debut CD entitled *"My Everything"*. Look for it soon. I am so sure you will be blessed by its contents.

Sisters of the Word Book Club
Los Angeles, CA
(Pictured from left to right: Rae Jones, Raena Banks, Adilah Barnes (author), Terry McNulty, Deborah Banks, Treva and DeBorah Pryor)

Deborah Banks
Educator– Former Government Employee–Avid Reader–
Coach– Student–Mentor

Although Deborah adamantly insisted I not include her in these writings, I could not complete this book without mentioning the role she has played in my success as well as in the successes of many others. Deborah would not share any information, but I know enough about her to give you some information.

Born the daughter of a preacher, Deborah is a former government employee, having worked for Social Security for many years. During her latter years at Social Security, she went back to school obtaining her master's degree, as her heart's desire was to move into education. Deborah now works in the school system, pursuing her purpose in helping disadvantaged youth accomplish their visions of obtaining a high school diploma but, more importantly, one of helping them become the best person they can be in every area—ministering to the whole person.

Currently residing in Inglewood CA, I am told she has been very involved in the goings-ons in her community— a voice for the people.

Being an avid reader for many years, she is a member, and possibly one of the founding members, of Sisters of the Word Book Club. The books read by these members have been many and very diverse.

Deborah has and continues to be involved with the Social Security Black Advisory Affairs Committee. Deborah is the gift that keeps on giving.

Deborah is a sports fanatic having been involved with softball for years, serving as a coach, encourager and motivator to the teams she's worked with.

She is very involved in her church, New Journey C.O.G.I.C., in Hawthorne CA, under the leadership of Pastor John Richardson.

Deborah is the mother of two daughters: the youngest of which is Raena Banks Neal, who is also a member of Sisters of the Word Book Club, and the older is Shanethia Neal aka "Shay". Raena, by the way, is an avid reader and a wonderful performer.

Deborah is so modest that trying to get information from her was probably worse than someone trying to pull her teeth. However, Ms. Deborah Banks, today I salute you. I aspire to be like you in many ways. As I pray and ask God to reveal people's hearts to me, all I can see in you is a heart of gold and a sincere desire to help people be the best they can be. For this I applaud you. You are not only my friend, my former co-worker, my former fellow book club member; you are my sister and I love you so much.

I thank God for having placed you in my life and pray that whatever you put your hands to do, God blesses you every step along the way.

Phenomenal woman! That's Deborah.

(Pictured Left to right: Regina Mixon, Linda Vincent and Terry McNulty)

Terry McNulty
Government Employee–Sisters of the Word Book Club Member

Sassy. Classy. Versatile. Devoted. Friendly. Humble. All of these are words that describe Terry McNulty. There are so many more that could be used. Suffice it to say another phenomenal woman.

Terry is married to Reginald "Reggie" McNulty Sr., and is the mother of two daughters, Jennifer and Christina and step-mother to "Little Reg" Reginald McNulty Jr. as well as mother to a special family member, Milo, their dog.

Terry is a member of Love and Unity Christian Fellowship where her pastor is none other than Pastor Ron C. Hill. It is because of her prodding that I became a member there; I actually became a member before she did.

A member of Sisters of the Word Book Club, the books that have been read are diverse and many.

Terry is also a fellow co-worker having worked for Social Security for many years.

When I first came to the Torrance Social Security office, Terry was one of the first people I met, and there was an instant bond. We joke from time to time that since we're both borderline insane the click was inevitable. However, it was much more; our spirits connected.

Terry has done so many wonderful things for my family and me over the years to show her genuine concern and love for us. When I had no car, she did not hesitate to give me rides to and from work and church. When I had no money, she graciously assisted in whatever way she could. When I just needed a friend, she was there. And for anyone who knows Terry, when a laugh was needed she was eager to oblige. That's Terry!

Terry is one of those women that are beautiful on the inside as well as the outside. Fabulous. Motivator. Encourager. Supporter. And I am happy to call her my friend.

Rae Jones
Executive Director, Great Beginnings for Black Babies,
Los Angeles–Sisters of the Word Book Club
www.gbbb-la.org

A trailblazing journalist and communications strategist, Rae Jones has spent the bulk of her thirty-five year professional career bringing attention to issues impacting the African American community. From health disparities to the disproportionate rate at which Blacks are impacted by domestic violence, autism and other developmental disorders, as well as the far-reaching and negative impact of the foster care and judicial systems, Ms. Jones has had hundreds of articles published over the years detailing the plight, as well as the highlights of African American life in the U.S. Ms. Jones currently serves as Executive Director of a twenty-year old Los Angeles-based nonprofit organization, Great Beginnings for Black Babies, which has a core mission of improving pregnancy outcomes for African American women, while also encouraging healthy lifestyles for families.

Prior to that, for three years Ms. Jones was Interim Executive Director for the Greater Los Angeles African American Chamber of Commerce, while also serving as its public relations firm of record under the auspices of her own company, Raediant Communications.

Most of her professional skills were cultivated in the broader Chicago Metropolitan area. However, for five years, Ms. Jones served as public affairs director for the Children's Bureau of Southern California in Los Angeles, and director of Public Relations and Communications for the Pasadena, CA-based Art Center College of Design.

In Chicago, Ms. Jones served as director of Public Relations for Malcolm X College, one of the City Colleges of Chicago; assistant press secretary to former Chicago Mayor Eugene Sawyer for whom she wrote speeches and coordinated issues and media campaigns; and, as director of Communications to the late Chicago Mayor Harold Washington, where she developed and implemented communications strategy for the City of Chicago.

Ms. Jones holds a Bachelor of Science degree in Journalism from Southern Illinois University/Carbondale and has taken postgraduate courses at Northern Illinois University and the University of California at Los Angeles (UCLA).

Another powerful Sister of the Word Book Club member and one I am proud to consider a friend.

Meme Kelly
www.memekelly.com
Author–Entrepreneur

While teaching elementary school for Los Angeles Unified School District and raising three sons, Meme Kelly self-published *On Edge*, a novel, and *Just Gotta Shout*, a spiritual affirmation book, selling thousands of copies in the U.S. With the support and guidance of freelance editors from two (2) major publishing houses, she recently completed her third book, *Wings to Fly*, a novel, and signed with a literary agency representing bestselling authors.

Meme is also the founder of Sisters Supporting Sisters, a non-profit organization dedicated to inspiring and serving young adults with special needs and women through the Principles of the SHOUT (Success, Hope and Happiness, Overcome Obstacles, Utilize God's Power, and Take Charge of Self). This life work was inspired by her desire to encourage and support her oldest son who has mild developmental delays and encourage other women to do their best. Through her non-profit efforts, Meme has done SHOUT seminars at inner city schools, women shelters, juvenile detention centers, community non-profits, book stores, coffee houses, and most recently, held a premiere event at a center for Young Adults with Special Needs. See also **Sisters Supporting Sisters** and **Just Gotta Shout**

She is a graduate of UCLA and resides in Sherman Oaks, California with her husband of 23 years and their three sons. Her life mission is to inspire, encourage and entertain through the written word and serve others through her non-profit efforts and inspirational 'SHOUT' seminars.

Meme regularly holds SHOUT events at various locations in the Los Angeles area. I have had the privilege of SHOUT'ing at a few sharing my testimony. Thanks Meme!

www.blackwomensnetwork.net
Sisters In Service To Enhance Resource Sharing

A "Women in Business Conference" was held at the Biltmore Hotel in downtown Los Angeles, attracting 2,000 women at the height of entrepreneurship and this new word "Networking". There were approximately two hundred African Americans in attendance at this mainstream event. Women passed the word, "like the call of the drum messages of long ago," that African American women were to meet at the end of the official conference day in a session room upstairs. At least eighty-five women heard the word and became the core group of what was to become known as **Black Women's Network (BWN)**.

We assembled our chairs in a large circle, which began our long-standing tradition of the "circle of introduction." The energy and excitement in the room was charged with the vitality of eighty-five corporate, business, and professional African American women who were often "the only one" in their companies. It was concluded that this positive energy and resource should be pursued.

Weeks later, we met at Exposition Park and continued our meetings at USC's Kerchoff Hall, where we continued to meet for the first year. We named our organization, developed our motto, established a dues assessment to fund our activities, formed committees, and with the skills of Marva J. Smith, our first elected president, formed by-laws. Prior to this, we selected a chairperson on a quarterly basis until we became more acquainted with each other and developed a clear organizational structure. Our first interim chairperson was Merna Mitchell, an executive with the UNCF. We met weekly, then bi-weekly that first year. Each month we grew in number, experience, structure, and wisdom. The growth experience of our first year truly established our motto as **Sisters In Service To Enhance Resource Sharing.** Our then vice-president, Mary Durham coined this phrase.

The initiation of a monthly newsletter took place with past president Lois Pitter-Bruce and Carole Wade Wharton as editors. A roster of members was also developed in a resource directory coordinated by past president Laura Odem. This directory became an essential networking tool that enabled members to purchase goods and services for each other, call on more experienced members for assistance, and connect with other women of similar personal interests.

The meetings became monthly, with agendas that included motivational seminars, workshops, networking sessions, and member-only business meetings planned to provide opportunity for closer interaction. We reached out to other women of color in Los Angeles with our first major all-day conference, "Getting There, Being There, Staying There," under then and now Conference Chairperson, Marva Smith Battle-Bey. With this annual fall event, BWN has launched into the community and has taken its place among existing organizations as a viable entity.

The Membership grew and the founding members were named as those women who were at the Biltmore session and as charter members those who joined within the first year. Our organization continues to not only serve its membership but also reaches out to the community to lend our efforts and talents to other women and young girls. We are…Sisters Standing Strong…**Black Women's Network.**

Proud to be a member of **Black Women's Network!**

Linda Ard-Bonner
2008—2010 President
Black Women's Network

Linda has served as president of Black Women's Network for fiscal years 2008– 2010. She is the owner of Linvitations, a business that does desktop publishing, event planning, favors and personalized keepsakes. She also does general accounting and non-profit accounting.

Linda is a natural motivator. One of the many gifts I've identified in her in the short time I've known her is that of encouraging others. Walking in the Black Women's Network was a pleasant experience from the very beginning due to the pleasantness, eagerness to help and the positive attitude of Linda Ard-Bonner.

Although a new president has been elected for 2011, Linda Ard-Bonner will continue to be an integral part of Black Women's Network.

Juanita Lane
2008–2010 Vice President
Black Women's Network

Born in San Francisco, California to Cedell (deceased) and Flora Lane, Juanita is such a joy to be around. She has one sibling, a brother, Ralph and no children, unless you count her two doggies ☺.

Juanita is an analyst working for the State of California as a Consumer Affairs Consultant. Juanita is a collector of Betty Boop articles, likes surfing the web, and is affiliated with Animal Rescue. She has a BA from San Francisco State University.

She is a member of Beebe Memorial Cathedral of Oakland, California.

Juanita has served since 2008 as vice president of Black Women's Network, membership chairperson and was chronicled in *"Who's Who in American Management"*.

Juanita is such a pleasure to be around. She has such a warm spirit and welcomes and embraces each new member into Black Women's Network. She, like Linda and I, instantly clicked or connected spiritually.

She is such a free spirit: fun-loving, passionate and committed to the cause, whatever it may be.

Juanita Lane is a shining light that brightens my day!

Michelle Moore-Bell
www.michellemoorebell.com
www.salon21-beauty.com

Michelle started her passion for the industry in 1981.

Her career started with graduating from Marinello Schools of Beauty in the Fairfax District of Los Angeles where she received hands-on training in Cosmetology.

She took an opportunity with Los Angeles' leading Salon "Simple Raw Hair Designers". She was trained by LaFay Davenport in the Simple Raw technique. She was also professionally trained at Dudley Cosmetology University in North Carolina. She continually receives advanced education in cutting, coloring, styling techniques and marketing. "With any career you can never stop learning; there are always new and innovative ideas to grow from." Over the years, Michelle has grown, exploring new and different ways to provide quality service and products. She is now educating and inspiring other beauty professionals.

In 1987 she opened Salon 21, after twenty-three years of providing a great place for other beauty professionals to work, learn and grow, along with providing quality customer service, products, producing an eight-page newsletter, and leading all you can be campaigns and a healthy lifestyle festival, she sold the business.

God has given Michelle another dream. As of April 5, 2010, she is still doing what she loves. but operating from another location and continuing to train others in the industry to live their dreams..

She continues to share the benefits of going to a professional and using professional take-home hair care products for healthy hair as well as the benefits of skin care and makeup application for women of all ages. As far as men's grooming, she provides special tips on make-up as it relates to film, television, fashion shows and editorial. In 1994, Michelle established The Wellness Group, a 501c(3) non-profit organization. They educate, inform, and empower women on breast health awareness and a healthy lifestyle.

Michelle's dream is about transforming the lives of women worldwide in the areas of beauty and wellness

Michelle introduced me to Black Women's Network. It was largely due to her invitation to one of their events that led me to become a member.

Another proud Black Women's Network member!

Joy Lewis-Anderson, The Networker

CEO, EnJOY PRomotions & Communications (c)—
www.enjoypromotions.webs.com

Founder of the 411 Cafe' Network
www.411cafenetwork.ning.com–Editor, The 411
Cafe' Newsletter –Jewel Diamond Taylor Associate

In some form or fashion I have been networking and sharing information since 1977 when I attended my first motivational seminar *"Why Not?"* in Manhattan Beach, California. I wanted to tell everyone I knew about this life-changing seminar. The "Why Not" seminar helped me to realize I wanted to live an extraordinary life. It was the beginning of discovering my purpose and passion. I always knew I wanted to work for myself but I didn't how to get started, "Why Not" was the trigger. My father, Robert Lewis owned a jewelry store in Washington, D.C. for over twenty-five years. His father, my grandfather, Robert Lewis, Sr. owned a general store and filling station in Vicksburg, Mississippi. Our father constantly reminded my sisters and myself to "work for yourself, be your own boss! "

From 1980 to 1984 my sisters and I hosted and coordinated the "Traveling Boutique" home shopping parties. We had found the perfect blend of taking care of business and socializing. We were "networking" before it became the "buzz" word for building a business. In 1984 I attended another life-changing motivational event presented by my favorite speaker and author, Jewel Diamond Taylor. Once again, I knew I had tapped into my life's purpose and passion.

In 1988 I produced my first of many "Business Expo" networking events at the Sheraton LAX Hotel. I was an active member of the **Business Builders Network** facilitated by the Master Networker, Mr. Bill McButts and part of the first telephone business network **"PhoneNet"** created by Ashiki Taylor and Prince Zaire. From 1994 to 2001 I traveled across the country and internationally with Jewel Diamond Taylor. It was exciting and a blessing to be part of the African-American Women on Tour Conferences presented by Maria Dowd as well as producing our events; Jewel Diamond Taylor's popular Sistefriends Retreats, Super Goal Saturday, and the Enlightened Circle and Women on the Grow events.

I love music, especially jazz! In 1999 I presented my first **"Jazz Cafe'"** event in Anaheim Hills, CA featuring the very talented jazz saxophonist, Mark "Panther" Felton. In 2002 I published my first online newsletter **"What's Going On?"** which is now **The 411 Cafe' Network**

Newsletter. In 2009 I launched the 411 Cafe' Business/Social Network. I enjoy hosting networking events that bring people together to share information, to get connected and enjoy quality entertainment. I like being part of a team and assisting and serving others to fulfill their goals.

I continue to work with Jewel Diamond Taylor aka "The Self-Esteem Dr." It's been a blessing and an amazing journey to be part of her ministry as she continues to empower, encourage and uplift her audiences. To learn more about Jewel Diamond Taylor please see her on YouTube.com and see her website link. Life is precious and time is a gift from God. It's never too late to tap in your purpose and passion. Always be true to yourself, see the beauty in life and be kind to others. Thank you again for visiting my online office and please remember to enjoy your day!

"A Meeting of the Minds Networking Group"
Los Angeles, California

Part 6
The Girlfriends

My Girls

Annette Jefferson and Others

Annette Jefferson, Sue McClendon Mason, Charlotte Mims-Williams, Doris Joyner, Kay Diane Caesar, Brenda Hawk, Shirley Winston Williams, Ethel Mae Miller, Ms. Claudia Adams, Mrs. Mozell Shelton aka "Mom" and Jennifer McKinney have proven themselves over the years to be true friends. Although Annette is the header name shown, each of them has proven to be invaluable for more than twenty years.

I could write an entire book about the many things we've done together. Suffice it to say that not only are they friends, they are family.

Each of these women has given tirelessly of themselves to many without any recognition or acknowledgement—not that they sought any. Though our lives have taken us in different directions, we are forever and will always be family.

These are beautiful women—inside and out —and I am proud to have had the opportunity to befriend them and grateful to acknowledge them in these writings.

Felonesecia Walker West
LPN– Student–Housewife– Mother– Arbonne Itl. Consultant

Felonesecia Walker West also known as D.I., has been a friend of mine for over twenty-five years. She has been a constant supporter, encourager, motivator, cheerleader, comforter—a real friend in the truest since.

Felonesecia is the wife of Rickie B. West (also profiled in these writings), the mother of two wonderful, talented daughters: Rickeythia and Darika West, and the grandmother of four: Kamron and Jeremiah, Princess and Amiah. She is the daughter of Mrs. Christine Herbert and the late Mr. Floyd Harper.

Felonesecia graduated from C. E. Byrd High School and currently attends Southern University, Shreveport

Louisiana where she is pursuing a degree to become a registered nurse.

She is employed with Meadowview Nursing Home in Minden, Louisiana where she utilizes her gifts of caring and helping those that are in need of twenty four–hour care, mainly the elderly and disabled.

Felonesecia is a member of the Mt. Calm Baptist Church in Minden, Louisiana where her pastor is the Rev. T. Alexander Knapp.

When not working or studying, she enjoys fishing, decorating, and talking. Many times I've referred to her as my bossy friend. I say this lovingly but for those that know her, you know that she can be just that. Her bossiness has helped propel me forward.

She says things like, "You can do it", "You're closer than you think", "How can I help you to make this happen?" and my all time favorite, "Get up and just do it". So, you see how her bossiness actually ended up helping me to believe that I could do anything and made me get up and do some things I did not want to but needed to do.

Felonesecia began in the natural products business October 14, 2006 as an Arbonne International Consultant. This is a wellness company that sells all– natural products that are pure, safe and beneficial containing no dyes, fillers or animal fat.

Felonesecia is a woman of purpose and determination in the real sense. Although not officially a registered member of the group, she is a woman on the go and a woman on the grow. Her philosophy on attaining anything is to never give up. She encourages everyone to take constant, consistent steps in pursuit of their purpose and often states that anyone can be as happy as they desire to be.

She is the epitome of a phenomenal woman.

Her favorite scripture is," But as it is written, Eye hath not seen, nor ear heard, neither have entered into the heart of man, the things which God hath prepared for them that love him." I Corinthians 2:9 KJV.

Look at the essay below on the following page to see why she chose to pursue nursing. You will see that she has a heart for people and truly understands the meaning of blessed to be a blessing. Felonesecia West—a real hero!

"How My Educational and Career Goals Will Help To Meet the Needs of the Elderly"

I've been an employee of Nexion Health for 13 years and there have been a lot of changes during my employment that makes me proud to work for this company. I have worked as a Licensed Practical Nurse for 10 years. Nursing is, for me, loving, caring, and giving of one's self; whatever obstacles I have encountered I know I will be successful in my nursing career. I chose nursing as my career because I wanted to make a difference in other's lives. I always wondered what I could do to make a difference and I felt that nursing was where I was needed to give the patients the help that they required.

I have been through some hard times in my life, having to deal with the death of my father, my grandmother, and the recent loss of my father- in –law. It is now time for me to, work hard, study and make my dreams come true. One thing I promised my father was to complete my education and to become a Registered Nurse. I am fortunate enough to be able to foresee ways of improving my nursing techniques. Obtaining my degree in nursing and becoming a Registered Nurse will help me even more to improve my techniques and assist my elderly patients by being a better advocate for them. Also, by enhancing my techniques, I will be able to enlarge my career and improve the quality of care given to my patients

Nursing has always been a lifelong dream ever since I was old enough to remember. After graduating High School, I worked several jobs before I decided it was time to fulfill my life long dream of becoming a nurse. I decided to go to school for LPN and now having the opportunity to return to school to complete my education to obtain my degree to become a RN. It was a challenging when I decided to return to school after being out of school for several years.

I would also like to mention that I was a Certified Nurses Assistant prior to becoming a LPN. Being a Certified Nurses Assistant was fulfilling but, I wanted more. After working as a Certified Nurses Assistant for about a year, I knew I had to make my dream a reality. Being a Certified Nurses Assistant gave me a chance to sit down talk, comb hair, dress and make my patients look great and have a feeling of self worth. There's a time when many families don't and can't visit and to the patients you are the only friendly face they see. When a patients smiles it brings joy and excitement to me and well as to the patient.

While working as a Certified Nurses Assistant there was a nurse I admired. She was caring, loved her residents, her job and was the nurse I wanted to be. After working in the nursing home for more than 13 years or so, I decided that I needed a change of environment. I started working for a hospice agency.

Hospice is for terminally ill patients, as well palliative care. The job consisted of taking care of terminally ill patients, patients with dementia and making sure that the patient does not suffer or die alone. This was a job that I enjoyed doing, because I felt the patient and their families needed me in their time of need as well as when they were grief stricken. The job gave me a feeling of self-worth and fulfilled my desire to be of service. I sat with the patient, kept them as comfortable as I possibly could, as well as informing and making them aware of what is going on with their families on the dying process of their loved one. I was fortunate enough to sit with patients in their homes and those that were already in long term care facilities.

Everyday I see more ways of improving my nursing skills to better serve my patients but I am restricted in so many ways because I am not yet a RN. Although, I have a ways to go, I am positive and determined to succeed.

Again, I chose nursing as my career goal because I wanted to make a difference in other's lives. Even as a small child I decided that I wanted to be able to help people. Also, as a child I wanted to become a nurse and I now have the opportunity to fulfill my life-long dream of becoming a RN. Now with help and much encouragement I will have the opportunity to give my patients my very best, by fulfilling my educational goals which would also improve my skills. Learning new skills and techniques will allow me to enhance the quality of life for the people that I care for on a day to day basis. Working hard and doing a good job is worth the time and effort.

RNs have the ability to bring about change that will benefit the patients as well as their families. Using my voice to advocate for my patients is a very important issue for me. The inability to perform an IV push, central line dressing changes, or administer blood means that my patients have to wait for a RN to be available. With only two RNs on duty for many patients it is sometimes difficult to get immediate care. Having my RN license will allow me to help alleviate some of the pressure being placed on the RNs we presently have on duty in our facility.

As an advocate for the patients, I will bring my experience from the floor as well as an understanding of the administrative aspect of nursing to the RN position. Hanging or monitoring Total Parenteral Nutrition (TPN) or blood for patients is reserved only for RN,s in most facilities. These life saving procedures are vital to patient care and having the knowledge and the capability to administer these procedures is just a small part of being an RN.

Part 7
The Brothers/Male Friends

Carlton Williams
Retired

Carlton A. Williams, born to Mr. and Mrs. Lonnie (Margaret) Williams of Minden, Louisiana and currently residing in Minden. Carlton has three living siblings, Stepfret, Linda, and Mary Ann; has been married twice and fathered several children.

While pursuing my involvement with God's Storehouse ministry in Minden, Louisiana, Carlton continually came to my rescue. Never once did he make me feel foolish about my mission or my beliefs; quite the opposite. Carlton brought me food, sat with me and talked for hours on end, provided me with small jobs to earn money (yes I mowed yards several times), helped me clear the property adjacent to the house that I had obtained and just did many things that are too numerous to mention. The main thing he did was continually be my friend and for that he will always and forever be my hero.

We had many candlelit dinners which he prepared at his place and brought to me—candlelit because the lights were off most of the times. ☺ But we had so much fun.

There were occasions where we argued as we differed on many subjects and I was so opinionated back then. And during those times, I would give him a piece of my mind (as if he cared). We would stop talking for a short while and he would be right back. That's love.

Carlton and I had a long history together before this all took place. I would be lying to say that all was great then. It wasn't. But through the years as we each matured we developed a mutual respect for each other and I came to know the man behind the mask.

Carlton has been someone who has helped many people during his lifetime. I have personally witnessed numerous occasions where he assisted someone and never received any recognition for doing so—not that he was looking for any; he just simply saw a need and met it.

I thank God for having the opportunity to recognize and acknowledge this man especially. It's long overdue. Carlton, did you ever know that you were my hero? I can fly higher than an eagle because you are the wind beneath my wings.

We fought. We laughed. We were lied on and misunderstood but in spite of it all, we made it. As you would often say to me, "tough times don't last but tough people do". Thank you for helping me to get tough.

Anthony A. Arline
Future Minister

Anthony Antwine Arline—Born the youngest of six children to Pastor Robert Arline Sr. and Annie Edwards Arline, both now deceased. Anthony was my second and third husband. Prior to our marriage, he was previously married and fathered three daughters.

Anthony was brought up in the word of God. In his quest for purpose in life he got off track and became involved in drugs. From an early age up until a short while ago he has battled with a crack cocaine addiction.

Anthony realized early in life that there was a calling by God to minister to hurting people. What he failed to realize was that in order to effectively reach other people's lives he would have to walk through much pains to get to a point of total surrender.

Jovial. Friendly. Loving. Fun-Loving. All of these can be words used to describe Anthony. Others are comforting, encouraging, and once he befriends someone he can become the best friend that person can have.

Anthony has always had a love for God. His desire has been to minister to people, telling of God's goodness and giving them hope. I'll now write what Anthony shared with me –

"I had a great upbringing and being in good relationships yielded me four beautiful daughters to include my step-daughter, Emily Mixon and my step-son, Kendrick J. Thomas. On August 30, 1997 and August 31, 2000 (?), God

gave me my queen, Regina Gale Mixon in matrimony. She treated me like her king.

I believe every man wants someone strong like their mom. Regina has all of the characteristics as my mom who was a strong Christian woman. The more I made her cry the stronger she became in the word of God and in the love of God.

I can truly say I have been loved unconditionally through her. She will always be my queen. I will always love her as my wife and friend. Gale, I am so proud of you.

During this period of incarceration and knowing what God has brought you from and through, I know God is no respecter of person. He did it for you and He will do it for me. Love always, your friend and ex-husband. Anthony A. Arline"

This is what Anthony wanted to share with you. Although these writings are not about me, I did say to those profiled that I would include whatever they submitted in the book.

Anthony, I thank you for being my friend, my encourager, my hero. I know that God is blessing you mightily and will honor your desire to reach many that are lost for His glory.

Anthony Antwine Arline, my hero.

Rickie B. West
Warehouse Supervisor, Coca-Cola Bottling Company

Rickie B. West is the son of Gladys Jones, the spouse of Felonesecia West and the father to Rickeythia and Darika West. Rickie has three siblings on his mother's side: Marlon, Ramona and Cedric and four additional siblings on his father's side: Willena, Romanea, Maurena and Alfred.

Rickie has been employed with Coca-Cola Bottling Company in Minden, Louisiana for more than eighteen years, working for approximately seventeen years as a truck driver. He currently serves as a warehouse supervisor.

Rickie is a graduate of Minden High School class of 1975.

Rickie has been a friend for more than twenty-five years and has assisted my family in so many ways. Not only has he done this but his entire family as well.

Sometimes one will say, especially a female, all I need is one good man. Even though he is married to one of my best friends, I found him to be on many occasions the one good man I needed.

Rickie has done so many things for us; I actually don't know where to begin. From fixing cars, to painting and repairing broken things, to installing ceiling fans, to helping clean and clear property—just name it and he's probably done it for us.

It's difficult sometimes to find someone that sticks with you through thick and thin: Rickie has been that someone.

He has counseled my son on numerous occasions in an attempt to teach him to become a man. Though it may have seemed that his words were falling on deaf ears, he continued to encourage and try to teach him. Not did he do this just for my son but for many young men.

His life early on was one of making many mistakes; however he learned from those and he quickly, eagerly shares his testimony with many to encourage them and to give God glory.

Now, there has been a time or two when he threatened to put me out of his house. ☺ At those times it was merely because I just didn't have sense enough to leave. Overall he's been nothing but a true friend.

Rickie, I say thank you and pray God's continued blessings over you and yours.

Travon Gilliam
Musician

I first met this young man when I relocated to California in 1989. At that time, he was a mere tot. He escorted my daughter to her very first debutante ball when she was age four and he was maybe six. Now today, after almost sixteen years, they are the proud parents of my wonderful grandson, Jordan Gilliam. Who would have thought?

Travon, or "T. J.", as we refer to him, has been so helpful to me personally during my stay in California since my return in 2003. I can always count on him to give me advice about car repairs, to assist me in my many moves and to just be there when I need a male's advice.

He has been employed in various capacities as a warehouse worker and a worker at a shoe repair shop, to name a few and is currently seeking gainful employment.

A gifted musician and vocalist, "T. J." plays drums like nobody's business.

"T. J., thank you for just being you. I know God has a bright future ahead for you. Keep the faith. The best is yet to come."

Paul Sabu Rogers
Producer–Director–Editor–Videographer
www.plazanoir.com

Paul Sabu Rogers', professional career in television production and film started in 1984, after a brief but productive career as a jazz and R&B musician. The music business took him from Chicago to New York, finally settling in Los Angeles in 1975, after tours with notable musical acts. This is where he became infatuated with the power of images to express creative ideas. After attending Pasadena City College and UCLA to become formally educated in the discipline of film and television media, Paul has worked steadily at honing his creative and technical sensibilities, from working as a cameraman for commercial production companies to editing, writing, directing, and producing for the government, corporate and entertainment marketplace.

Paul has been responsible for the creative production of hundreds of presentations which range from television commercials, music-videos, cable television programming, electronic press kits, and dramatic shorts and documentary film projects, just to name a few. Many of Paul Sabu's projects have been administered through his production company, BMV Productions. As the CEO and founder of BMV Productions he has been able to gardner a impressive array of clientele, while establishing a reputation for quality, effective and affordable media services.

Currently, he is combining his talents with other inspired collaborators from Oscar award winning filmmakers to Grammy nominated artists to create original content for independent distribution. You will find many of these collaborators and partners taking advantage of his marketing and advertising web portal, Plaza Noir Inc. Plazanoir.com is the realization of Paul's long time dream to create an outlet for businesses to bring their media message to the a mass market. Today, Mr. Rogers is fulfilling that dream and his entrepreneurial vision.

It is none other than Paul Rogers who is the director/producer and behind the scenes person for my book trailer for *"To God be the Glory"*. First introduced to him by another person profiled, DeBorah Pryor, I felt totally and completely at ease in doing this project with him. I walked away from our initial meeting knowing that God had once again given me His best. I was not wrong.

Michael Riddick

Photographer

"Michael Riddick is often found on the red carpet, shooting celebrities. He also shoots head shots and the usual photo packages, but don't ask him to do weddings. Michael Riddick would much rather comb the streets of Los Angeles for the issues of the day.

Michael has seen some of everything through the eyes of his camera: crime, police brutality, and black and brown wars.

"I feel the need to show the real side of the problems we have. I know a lot of guys don't like it, but for some reason I have this drive and I can't explain it, but those families touch me deeply. I want people to know the real side that only this camera and I can show. Sometimes I get scared myself, because you have to read the people's hearts and it hurts, but I want to show people who don't want to face the real, even if it scares me to see it."

Michael has shot event photography for many activist organizations including the Brotherhood Crusade, Pathways to Your Future and gang intervention programs."

(Excerpt from www.expoupdate.com)

Michael has served as my personal photographer for more than three years. He is always available for photo shoots whenever I call upon him. And, if by chance he has something previously scheduled, he immediately pens me in. That, to me, means much.

He is a professional in the truest sense and takes what he does very seriously.

Michael, I thank God that Vicki Phillips of The Bio Shop introduced me to you. The relationship has proven to be one I will cherish wherever I go. I absolutely love working with people who love what they do. It's so obvious you are one of those people—the camera doesn't lie.

Robert Nubine
Dancer–Upcoming Author

To Robert Nubine, dance is a natural form of artistic expression. A native of Los Angeles, he grew up performing in dance halls alongside his mother, an "entertainment illusionist." While attending Gardena High School (from which he later graduated), he started the "Get Krump Crew," a street dance team featuring freestyle, high energy hip hop dance moves. Robert says, "I am a versatile dancer. In addition to hip hop, I love modern and jazz dance because of the way in which I am able to use my arms." His love for all types of dance led him to collaborate with four others to start "Hydration," a dance crew with a fluid, jazzy flavor. A spiritually grounded person, Robert also uses his talents to share God's message. As a former member of "Here2Prayze," he interprets traditional and contemporary gospel music with his church's liturgical dance ministry. The twenty-three year old says that dance has served as a positive outlet of expression, which has enabled him to cope with difficult circumstances. These trials and tribulations as well as the resultant triumphs and hope form the bedrock of the testimony that he enjoys sharing with others. Robert is also a singer, who has performed with choirs and vocal ensembles. While this young man is multi-talented, he says that dance is his passion as well as his ministry.

Robert is yet another young man that I met and came to love since my move to California in 2003. As a close friend of my daughter, he has gone through many ups and downs with us. He is another God-given son.

As I stated earlier, I've moved a few times since 2003 and Robert has been there packing and moving things through each one. He is Jordan's "Tonkon" instead of uncle. ☺

Anyone who knows me knows that I can be very long-winded meaning I talk a lot. I've felt so sorry for Robert as he would sit for hours at a time—in pain I'm sure—while I ranted and raved about any and everything. When my daughter had sense enough to leave, Robert stayed. For that and so many other things, I say thank you. You are my son and my super hero.

Henry W. Harris Sr.
www.spiritco1.com

Henry W. Harris is President of Spirit Telecommunications Company, Spirit is a voice and data communications company founded in the state of Maryland in 1995 and located at 6178 Oxon Hill Road Suite 101 Oxon Hill, Maryland 20745.

Henry W. Harris Sr. Currently serves on the Prince Georges County, Maryland Solid Waste Advisory Commission and the Prince Georges County Minority Business Opportunity Commission.

Henry W. Harris Sr. is active with community organizations, life time member of the South County Economic Development Association and political liaison for the Sunrise Homeowners Association.

In 2003 Henry W. Harris Sr. founded the Christian Internet Radio Service Spiritco1. Spiritco1 was created to give Christian artists an outlet to broadcast to the world using internet technology.

For the past 20 years Henry has been involved in the technology, community and business industry working in some capacity.

He has brought his wealth of experience to bridging the gap in small business and community to cooperative levels.

Henry's expertise and training has won him numerous awards, certificates and citations. Man of the year with the Greater Mt. Calvary Holy church in Washington, DC.
Henry has supported the Gospel Music Stellar Awards both as a sponsor of events and as a member of the Stellar Awards Gospel Music Academy Advisory Board.

As President of the board, Henry has developed ideals and tasks to help the organization grow its membership and maintain the membership base currently in place.

In addition to Henry's busy and active scheduled his is very involved in several community and church related activities, helping to empower the community.

Henry W. Harris Sr. Summary Membership Organizations

- Small Business Owner, Spirit Telecommunications Company, Oxon Hill, Maryland since October 1995.

- Member, Prince Georges County Black Chamber

- Boy Scout Computer Merit Badge Instructor

- Maryland Top 100 Minority business Enterprise Award 2007

- Former Member The National Capital Minority Business Opportunity Committee 2004

- Small Business of the Year. Prince Georges County Public Schools. 1999

- Life Business Member South County Economic Development Association

- Graduate of Prince Georges Community College, Business Management Degree 1987

I honestly can't remember exactly how Henry and I connected (I believe it was through facebook). I can say that everything afterwards has been a real pleasure. It is because of Henry that I became a member of the Stellar Awards Gospel Music Academy and attended my first Stellar Awards in Nashville in 2010.

After Angela Wills' completion of the song for my book trailer, *To God be the Glory*, it was none other than Henry Harris who gave her playtime on his radio station. I'll never forget the excitement when her name was shown on his playlist on facebook next to some world-renowned singers. She called me and said, "Is that my name next to Hezekiah Walker?"

Henry is a visionary whose dreams are to help others achieve their goals, visions, and dreams. He is a server.

I therefore, the prisoner of the Lord, beseech you that ye walk worthy of the vocation wherewith ye are called. With all lowliness and meekness, with longsuffering, forbearing one another in love; Endeavoring to keep the unity of the Spirit in the bond of peace. There is one body, and one Spirit, even as ye are called in one hope of your calling.

Ephesians 4: 1-4

Part 8
My Dream Team

Emily Mixon

Dancer–Upcoming Author–
REGS Books Founding
Member–Student

A famous modern dancer and choreographer, Martha Graham, once said, "Dance is the hidden language of the soul of the body." And, Emily Mixon shares that belief. Grounded in faith and inspired by God, the young woman expresses her creativity and spirituality through her dance moves. As a former member of Here2Prayze, liturgical dance ministry at The Word of God Missionary Baptist Church, the young adult uses her arms and legs to gracefully interpret the traditional and contemporary gospel music to which she performs. As a young person growing up in Minden, Louisiana, she developed an interest in arts education, partly, she says, to cope with the struggles of her early life. While in school, she excelled in choir, dance and even played the drums. After moving to Los Angeles in 2003, she attended and later graduated from Jordan High School. While at Jordan, however, she made the decision to concentrate her artist pursuits on dancing, specifically modern dance and hip hop, with the hope of becoming a professional dancer. Active in her church, Emily believes that through her dance ministry, she can share with young people, the value of artist expression in coping with life's obstacles.

Emily is my daughter and my pride and joy. The mother of one son, Jordan D. Gilliam, Emily has endured many hardships growing up, largely due to the mistakes made by her mother. Although her life is still not where she wants it to be, she has come to recognize and realize that she is a work in progress.

Emily has worked tirelessly over the past few years giving of her time, money and talents to help me pursue my visions and dreams. She has been doing an internship with REGS Books over the past few years learning all of the various aspects of book publications and marketing strategies often for little or no pay.

Loving, kind, giving, and optimistic are all words that can be used to define Emily. She is a young woman of faith consistently taking steps daily to improve her life while helping others. She is one I am proud to call my daughter.

Gail Marie Hughes King
Asst. Manager, Social Security Administration–Mother–Teacher–REGS Books Founding Member

Gail Marie Hughes was born to Maurice I. and Vera M. Hughes, in February 1955, in Washington, D. C. where she attended public schools through the eighth grade. She has one brother, Maurice, Jr. She attended Zion Baptist Church weekly and became a devoted youth usher. She joined the Camp Fire Girls of America as an active member for six years and went to camp each summer for four to six weeks. The entire family was involved in scouting – Father was a Scoutmaster, Mother was a Camp Fire Girl Leader, and Brother was a Cub Scout and then a Boy Scout. Gail studied the piano for six years. As a teenager, she participated in the Junior Democrats organization. Her family moved to Rockville, Maryland, where she completed her education and graduated after the eleventh grade, in August 1972. While in high school, Gail worked in the school library, joined and participated in the Conservation Club, Debate Club, Chess Club, Science Club and Mathematics Club. It was in high school where she began giving intensive tutoring to other students, both formally in classes and informally outside of school.

Gail studied mathematics and biochemistry as her double major for three years at the University of California at Los Angeles, UCLA. While at UCLA, she annually participated in the Uni Camp Fundraiser project, UCLA's Mardi Gras. Additionally, one summer she worked at Uni Camp as a counselor for disabled and underprivileged campers. She worked in a real estate office, while in college and would later earn her real estate license.

Gail married Garry L. King in August 1979 in Los Angeles, California. Garry is a Division Supervisor at Los Angeles International Airport, LAX and the Chairman of the Deacons' Ministry at The Word of God Missionary Baptist Church. Together they have five adult children, Garry, Jr., Latasha, André, Charles and Ligia. Their children grew up, attended and served in The Word of God Missionary Baptist Church and completed their high school education in Los Angeles Public Schools. Garry, Jr. and Charles are on active duty in the United States Air Force. Garry, Jr. has married Gabriela Zelaya (adding a third daughter); the family is stationed in North Carolina. Charles is stationed in South Korea and will be reassigned to Italy soon. Latasha graduated from University of Tennessee at Memphis as Dr. Latasha M. King, Pharm D, and is practicing in Tennessee, Mississippi, and California. André graduated from DeVry University at Long Beach, California, majoring in Computer Networking Systems, and is currently managing the electronic media services department for attorney firms, at his company in Century City, California. Ligia graduated from California State University at Northridge, CSUN in June 2009, in biochemistry. She desires to work in forensics. Garry &

Gail are extremely proud of all of their children, their accomplishments and celebration of their lives.

Gail began her public sector career in August 1975, with the Social Security Administration, as a Teleservice Representative. She has held positions as Technical Assistant, Teleservice Supervisor, Operations Supervisor, Assistant District Manager and temporarily District Manager. She has received numerous performance awards and special act awards. She has notably rendered special talent in training within the agency, participating in several training cadres throughout her career.

Mrs. King has been extremely active in the Boy Scouts of America program since September 1991 with Cub Scout Pack 566 and Boy Scout Troop 566, in Los Angeles, California. She has continuously been the Cub Master since 1992 and also the Scout Master since 2000. During this time, the pack and troop have served a few hundred boys and their families, in a minority, multicultural, at-risk community where they have learned life skills and prepared for adulthood. Many of these youth have been helped by having after school and weekend activities and by having a choice of group interaction through scouting, instead of gangs. The Cub Scout pack has had active membership from six to forty-five and the Boy Scout troop has had active membership from five to twenty at various times in the past seventeen years. Gail has provided an avenue for these youth to participate in trips, camping, hiking, fishing, cross-country and downhill skiing, boating, bowling, basketball, bicycling, community service, horseback riding, four months of swimming lessons each year, and much more.

The major annual community project Mrs. King's units participate in is the *Scouting for Food Plus* event in November. Consistently, Gail's Scouts collect over one ton of food and over fifty boxes of clothes for children and adults, all on one Saturday. After the collections, these items are sorted, categorized and redistributed to community centers that take care of the community's indigents' clothing and hunger needs.

Gail led her Pack and Troop 566 to be big brother units to a newly formed pack and troop whose members were disabled. The four units worked side-by-side to give assistance, guidance and training to the handicapped Scouts. All of the youth benefited in this exchange of goodwill.

One of the many services that Gail has offered her Scouts and youth at her church (and their siblings or other relatives) is free academic tutoring twice a week. These students, ranging from elementary to adult education, receive assistance in any academic subject, as needed, from Mrs. King. The attendance at these two day-a-week classes has ranged in attendance from one up to twelve students, at one time. Gail also has one-on-one tutoring sessions as desired and required by the students' needs outside of the regularly scheduled classes. Students learn basic study skills, basic academic subjects, computer skills, and some advanced subjects such as trigonometry, calculus, chemistry, and biology. Gail began tutoring when it became clear that many of the youth were not achieving academic success and needed help. She believes that our youth must receive balance in their exposure and growth, and that balance is obligated to include strong academic learning. All of her students are minorities from the low economic, inner city community, where the schools are struggling to elevate students to learn and achieve at their own grade levels.

Mrs. King is equally active in her church activities at The Word of God Baptist Church, located in South Central Los Angeles, having been a member since August 1972. She currently teaches Sunday school children's class, serves as an usher, coordinates the administrative ministry, serves as Christian Education Director and has served as the pastor's Executive Assistant. One of her passions is the Outreach Ministry, which provides free hot meals, clothing and toiletry items to the homeless and needy. Gail participates in serving breakfast each Sunday morning between 8:00 A.M. to 9:00 A.M., and then serving hot lunches twice a month on Saturdays beginning at 2:00 P.M. When the Outreach Ministry provides the free giveaways, Gail is there to assist in the distribution to the homeless. Currently, the Sunday morning breakfast program feeds between forty-five and sixty individuals each week. The Saturday feeding program serves approximately thirty individuals each of the two Saturdays.

The most recent adventure Gail has embarked upon is the HOPE HUMAN RESOURCE CORP., which prepares and links unemployed individuals with employers. She interviews, counsels and advises potential employees as to the best practices of gaining employment.

Gail helped to start REGS, through strong, unrelenting encouragement to Regina Mixon that she should follow her dreams, visions and goals! Many hours of loving discussion ensued, and REGS was born. Gail is proud to be a part of and to give support to REGS!

Gail loves the Word of God, the Body of Christ, education, music, the outdoors, driving, theater, and her *family* – immediate and extended - by birth, adoption, or marriage!

Gail is someone who has been nothing but a friend from day one. I have learned over the years to be careful who you consider a friend—she's proven herself countless times by putting her money, time and resources where her mouth is. She walks the walk.

I jokingly refer to her as being high-strung and neurotic. As you can see by all of the things she does and has done she is just a mover and a shaker.

I can always count on Gail to impart words of wisdom into my life. A true friend, a family member and most definitely a hero.

Shyeta J. Mozeke
Personal Assistant to Regina Mixon, REGS Books—
Student

Shyeta Jean Mozeke born to Celita Wright and Jeffery Mozeke, May 23, 1991 in Los Angeles, California.

Shyeta has one sibling, Darryl Jerome Sullivan.

Shyeta exemplifies the epitome of a virtuous woman in the makings. Having endured the loss of her mother at an early age, she has encountered many emotional hardships. Not to be swayed or discouraged by her lot in life, she is currently attending UEI to further her education pursuing a career in the medical profession.

Because Shyeta's mother passed away in July of 1997, Shyeta was raised by her grandmother, Dorothy Mozeke.

Baptized in June of 2005, Shyeta loves attending church services and is a member of the Greater Zion Church Family of Compton, California, under the leadership of Dr. Michael J. T. Fisher.

Hobbies and interests include playing tennis, writing, reading, singing, dancing, and talking. She enjoys watching movies, shopping with friends, going to school and "just being a teenager."

"I'm Shyeta, the girl that loves to make other people laugh; the girl that is not the smartest or the brightest but is far from what others proclaim me to be. I'm not perfect and I've made a lot of mistakes, but this is not the end. I can. I must. I will make it.

Shyeta Jean Mozeke: nurse, singer, actor, millionaire in training, wife and mother."

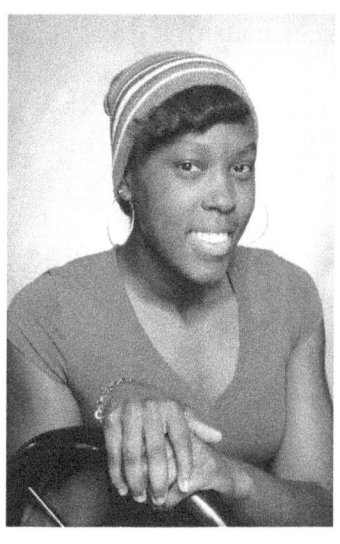

Victoria L. Gipson
Administrative Assistant, REGS Books Founding Member–Student

Poetry writer, basketball player, and dancer are some of the words that can be used to describe Victoria LaRae Gipson. Victoria, or Vicki, serves as the Administrative Assistant for REGS Books.

Other hobbies and interests she has are: braiding hair and working with computers.

Vicki is the daughter of Veleka White and William White (step-dad). She has two siblings: Marvin, age 13 and Raymond, age 12.

She is a member of the Greater Zion Baptist Church in Compton, California, under the leadership of Dr. Michael J. T. Fisher.

A 2006 Locke High graduate, Vicki aspires to do many great things in life.

Vicki has worked with REGS Books over the past couple of years wearing many hats. Her primary function is serving as Administrative Assistant.

Her gifts and talents continue to be a great asset to this ever-expanding company.

When Vicki came into our lives we were still going through. Once she became a part of our family she went through right along with us—never complaining. She has been an extension of my right hand for three years at least always available to do whatever needs to be done. Normally the service is with a smile.

Vicki is my god-daughter, my friend, my leaning post, my sounding board, and I am eternally grateful to God for having blessed me with yet another wonderful daughter.

God truly blessed us in the person of Victoria Gipson. Grateful comes to mind.

Linda R. Kinchelow
USC Office of General Counsel, Administrative Services Coordinator II/Paralegal–
REGS Books Advisory Board/Founding Member

Who would have thought a chance meeting on a bus would provide me with a friend for many years afterwards? Well, I found that friend in Linda Kinchelow.

I must admit, when I first met her I thought she was stuck up. Don't worry; I told her this many times. Was I wrong? Yes!

Linda Kinchelow: committed, caring, motivated, exciting, dependable, anointed, prayer warrior, all describe Linda. Linda is an employee in the Legal Department at the University of Southern California. She has worked in this field for more than nineteen years.

Linda is the mother of three: Marika, Nakita, and Edwin, Jr. and the proud grandmother of eleven.

Linda is active in the St. Matthew Baptist Church in Los Angeles where her pastor is Rev. Charlie B. Green, Jr. She serves as an advisor to the youth and young adult usher board, a member of the board of trustees, and she assists wherever there is need in the church.

Linda's plans include returning to school and pursuing a degree in the field of Administration (Childcare Development).

Born in Mississippi, Linda and her family moved to Memphis TN when she was around age four. Migrating to Los Angeles afterward having marrying the love of her life, Edwin V. Kinchelow, Sr.(now deceased), she began a new life.

Linda is knowledgeable in so many areas and is an anointed prayer warrior. She believes in the power of prayer and knows beyond a shadow of a doubt of God's existence. She is not ashamed to give God the glory for everything that's happened in her life and encourages others to develop a relationship with Him.

It's largely due to Linda that I started to pray the prayer for wisdom, knowledge and understanding. I noticed she included this in her prayers often when we came together and prayed. Now I include it in mine knowing that with this three one cannot go wrong.

Linda is one who when I had no transportation, she was there taking me to get nails done, to a speaking engagement in San Diego, shopping, wherever I needed to go, and I do not take that lightly. She stepped in at a time that I needed a friend the most and she's still here for me and I for her.

Suffice it to say that Linda Kinchelow is another she-ro of mine. Like some of the other women mentioned in this book, she serves as my mentor, coach, driver, friend, encourager, prayer partner, and friend. Yes, another shero!

Anita J. Williams
Social Security Administration Employee–REGS Books Advisory Board

"Will the Real Anita Williams Please Stand Up?"

A native Texan, born and raised in West Texas, where I attended Western Texas College. The eldest of a total of twelve children, including many from blended families. After attending college, I got married and moved to Odessa, Texas where I became the mother of three wonderful children—a handsome son and two beautiful daughters.

My greatest inspirations while growing up were four very important ladies in my life. My number one inspiration was my grandmother, Rosie Turner, who taught me to love unconditionally and trust in God and to treat everyone with patience and kindness. My mother, Jearldene Anderson, who still resides in west Texas, taught me that hard work and diligence always pays off and to study hard and I could become anything I want —there is no limit on the things one can accomplish.

My aunt, Dorothy Garcia, was one of my other favorite inspirations. She taught me how to laugh and to live and enjoy life on my own terms. She also taught every niece and nephew as well as grand nieces and nephews how to be the best "darn" domino players in west Texas.

My last, but not least favorite lady was my cousin/aunt, Norma Archie, who taught me faith—that anything is possible with God and no matter how small or large your request is God can and will provide.

One thing I discovered while my children were growing up is that you are never too young to teach people something. My son, Marcus, was my right arm—we seem to have grown up together. Many times as he got older and I was going through things, he always had a word of wisdom and he was always able to turn a bad situation into something that you would later have to laugh about. He was my hero and the *"wind beneath my wings"*. He kept me inspired to "keep on keeping on" even when I wanted to quit. I miss him dearly—God called him home about ten years ago and even through my loss of him he was still teaching me how to be strong. May he rest in peace until we meet again.

My middle child and oldest daughter, Nikki, taught me to have lots of patience and understanding and to always expect the unexpected and just to laugh a lot.

My youngest child and baby girl, Kim, taught me to give lots of hugs and plenty of kisses. Her favorite thing to say growing up was "I love you this much", as she spread her arms as wide as she could. She also taught me to believe in myself no matter how bad things were and never give up.

While living in Odessa, I had the privilege of meeting an amazing and blessed man and woman of God, Elder James and Carolyn Porter of Walker Chapel C.O.G.I.C. I had the privilege of sitting under their ministry and guidance and I credit them with helping me to get my life on the right track and continuing to guide me on this journey with the Master.

After living in Odessa for about sixteen years, I decided that it was time to move on to bigger and better places. I moved to the Dallas area where I resided for ten years before moving to the Long Beach area.

I have a background in customer service training and I am currently employed with the Social Security Administration, where I had the honor of meeting Ms. Regina Mixon. Meeting Regina has been a true blessing. She is a talented, caring, and awesome "warrior" woman of God.

Two favorite quotes I try to pattern my life by come from my pastor in the Dallas area of Elevate Life Church, "Elevate your thinking and elevate your life" and "Think, Be, Do!" You have to think it before you can be and then you have to be it before you can do it. Proverbs 3:5-6 also has special meaning in my life—"Trust in the Lord with all your heart…"

May REGS Books and family have an Ephesians 3:20 blessing.

I look forward to working with what sounds like an amazing group of women.

"If your dream can be achieved by you alone your dream is not big enough. Great dreams demand great teams."

Absolutely awesome woman of God! My sister in Christ, my encourager, my supporter, my teacher, my friend—Anita J. Williams!

Felicia Tatum
Social Security Administration Employee–REGS Books Advisory Board

I was born and raised in Long Beach California. I am the youngest of 3 siblings. I attended Cal State Dominguez Hills and graduated in 2000 majoring in psychology and a minor in behavior science. Once I graduated I began my career with the Federal Government at the Social Security Administration in September of 2003. In 2005, I decided to continue my education by resuming my master's degree. In 2007 I graduated from the University of Phoenix with a degree in business/public admin. In 2007 I also got married to a wonderful man named Rushan January we have been married for three year and we are eagerly awaiting the arrival of our baby daughter on Feb. 2, 2011. I am currently in the process of starting a family owned day care center early next year. My duties with the daycare will be assistant manager and advertiser for the center.

Felicia has served on the Advisory Board of REGS Books since 2009. Her testimonial is also shown on the book trailer for *"To God be the Glory"*. Felicia is a phenomenal woman and a great asset not only to REGS Books but to many.

With the upcoming birth of her first child, Felicia has informed us she will not be able to be as involved as in the past; however we hope she'll return, and we wish her family the best.

Felicia Tatum, you are and will forever be my hero—our hero! Thanks for being you.

Minister Shanta' Goodrum
Sales Director, REGS Books–Cannon Employee

Shanta' Goodrum is a career-driven young woman. With a resume that houses ten years of experience in sales and marketing, as well as being an ordained minister; she is truly a driving force to be reckoned with.

Shanta' is very passionate about getting and producing major results in both a career and in ministry. Since her 2003 national ordination with Christ Full Gospel Ministries, Shanta' has traveled to various parts of the USA preaching the word of God.

In 2005 she founded Full Gospel Evangelistic Ministries, an organization that helps people find themselves back to Christ while promoting self empowerment. Full Gospel is currently preparing to wear its new robe in the world of real estate.

In 2007 New Age Electronics deemed her the Sales Representative of the Year because she produced record breaking numbers. In 2010 Shanta' joined the family of REGS Books. Shanta' Goodrum is truly a go-getter and she is looking forward to helping with the success of the endeavors of REGS Books.

Shanta' is currently gainfully employed with Cannon in sales. Once REGS Books is fully up and running, Shanta' will serve as the company's sales director.

Shanta' is another trooper committed to the cause.

Onekia H. Mixon
Student–REGS Books Newsletter Editor

Onekia Mixon served as our newsletter editor in 2010. Her hard work helped us spread news of interest to many. Her dedication and willingness to learn the job helped launch REGS Books to yet another level. She was behind the scenes performing the tasks while many credited me with the work. This writing exposes the real person performing the work.

Onekia is my niece and currently a senior at Minden High School in Minden, Louisiana, graduating May 2011.

She is the daughter of Bruce and Della Mixon and has one younger sibling, Ladarrian Mixon.

Onekia attends Greater New Zion in Benton, Louisiana under the leadership of Pastor Donald Anderson.

Her plans are to pursue a college education with aspirations of becoming a medical doctor.

Thank you, Neka, for all of your hard work and efforts. We could not be where we are today without your assistance. Thank you for your belief in my vision enough to give of yourself to the cause. I love you much!

Kendrick J. Thomas
Incarcerated–REGS Books

Kendrick J. Thomas, my God-given son. Born to Chrisetta Thomas, September 5, 1980 in Shreveport, LA., Kendrick became my son not long after his birth. Kendrick has four biological siblings: Dwight, LaShonda, LaVerne aka "Pookey" and Marvin and one other sister, Emily Nicole Mixon. Not only did Kendrick become a part of my family but later his mother and siblings did as well.

Kendrick is married to Keisha Fuller Thomas and the father of two beautiful daughters: Kimmerlie and Khrystal Regina Thomas.

Currently incarcerated in Louisiana, Kendrick has had many mishaps since age 14. Trying to find his way, Kendrick ended up making many bad decisions as many of us have. His biggest mistake was in not believing his life could be different in positive ways.

Kendrick came into my life at a time God knew I needed him. His coming helped save my life and I thank God for giving him to me. By coming into my life at such a young age and when I was really on the road to destruction, I realized I had someone else that I was responsible for and knew that I had to make some serious changes.

He went through the many bad decisions I made and endured a lot. As a parent, I did what I thought was best and made a lot of mistakes. Through it all he loved me in spite of me and forgave me for all.

Kendrick is currently a partner with REGS Books and upon his release from jail will walk into the ministry God has given this family that consists partially of sharing our testimonies, encouraging and assisting others.

Kendrick Jermaine Thomas, my son and forever my hero.

Part 9
Conclusion

❧ Conclusion ❧

"Glory Wind Beneath My Wings" is the third book in a four-part series deemed the *"To God be the Glory"* series. As stated in the introduction, this book profiles *some* of my unsung heroes. It was and is humanly impossible to profile each and every person that has had a positive influence in my life. Please know that omission of your name and profile does not in any way diminish my appreciation to you for the roles you've played in my success.

Projects, visions and dreams that were dormant for many years began to resurface largely due to the encouragement I received from those profiled. I began to believe that I could accomplish anything, and I say "thanks."

It would be an insult and an outrage not to include my hometown and the people therein: the city of Minden, Louisiana. Growing up in "The Friendliest City in the South" and being nurtured by the many teachers, elders, and family members, has taught me invaluable lessons, lessons I will carry with me for the rest of my life. "Be it ever so humble, there is no place like home". (1822 *"Home, Sweet Home!"* Payne and Bishop)

In my first book, *"To God be the Glory"* I shared my journey of going from brokenness to wholeness. I shared with you visions, dreams, and promises given by God. *"Pursuing Your Purpose with Passion"* provided eight practical steps to live life better than ever before and S.O.A.R. *"Glory Wind Beneath My Wings"* acknowledges some of my heroes. Look for the upcoming book and the last in this series, *"The Manifested Glory of God"*. This one may take some time before its actual publication as during this season God will manifest the promises given.

Finally, I do encourage you to take the time to thank and acknowledge those that have been instrumental in your successes in life. People do need to know that they've made a difference. Don't wait until it's too late—do it now!

Each of those profiled, although separated by categories, can be lumped into one category that says it all—family. I thank God for all of you. *To God be the Glory!*

> Make new friends but keep the old ones; one is silver and the other is gold.

www.ingramcontent.com/pod-product-compliance
Lightning Source LLC
Chambersburg PA
CBHW072336300426
44109CB00042B/1633